HOME EXCHANGING
The Complete Source Book For Travelers At Home And Abroad

James Dearing

The East Woods Press
Charlotte, North Carolina

© 1986 by Fast & McMillan Publishers, Inc.
First printing.

All rights reserved. No part of this book may be reproduced without permission from the publishers, except by a reviewer who may quote brief passages in a review; nor may any part of this book be reproduced, stored in a retrieval system or transmitted in any form or by any means, electronic, mechanical, photocopying, recording or other, without permission from the publisher.

Library of Congress Cataloging-in-Publication Data

Dearing, James W.
  Home exchanging.

  Includes index.
    1. Hotels, taverns, etc. — Directories.   2. Vacation homes — Directories
  I. Title   II. Title: Complete sourcebook for travelers at home and abroad.
  TX907.D35   1986   647'.94   85-45694
  ISBN 0-88742-063-X
  ISBN 0-88742-074-5 (pbk.)

Cover design by Kenn Compton

Typography by R & J Publishing Company
Printed in the United States of America

East Woods Press Books
Fast & McMillan Publishers, Inc.
429 East Boulevard
Charlotte, NC 28203

Home Exchanging

The Complete Source Book For Travelers At Home And Abroad

SMU LIBRARY

What This Book Can Do For You

Have you dreamt of living somewhere else? Switzerland perhaps? How about Spain or Japan? Or would a country in North or South America be more to your liking?

Go ahead, choose. By exchanging homes your choice can become reality over and over again.

Exchanging homes can be the answer when the cumulative cost of transportation, lodging, eating, and entertainment makes traveling prohibitive. And it can be an exciting adventure for those people bored by superficial vacations, those wanting to probe deeper, to learn more and to experience more.

Although home exchanging is not the answer to everyone's travel and accommodation needs, it does offer unique advantages over other means of traveling and staying away from your home; the sublime dividend being the experience of living as a resident within another society and culture.

For beginners this book explains the philosophy of exchanging, how to effectively advertise with or without exchange agencies, how to investigate your potential partners to insure their integrity, how to complete the deal, and how to prepare for your exchange.

For experienced exchangers this book serves as a reference guide to assist you in contacting people not normally listed in agency catalogs, assuring that your exchange options continue to increase and enhance your travel life. Two of the three Appendices list agencies, major newspapers, colleges and universities, community host organizations, international associations, and other sources throughout the world to enable you to contact more exchangers.

Thousands of people exchange their homes every year and see their travel dreams come true. You can too.

Acknowledgements

This book was only completed after several lengthy delays that, though certainly frustrating, nevertheless have contributed to the book's conceptualization and completeness.

I wish to thank the agency organizers affiliated as INTERVAC International for allowing me to sit in during their 1983 annual meeting in Drogheda, Ireland, and to the host of that event, Frank Kelly, for introducing me to one of Ireland's finest and oldest pubs. The cooperativeness of all the organizers was appreciated.

My wife Rebecca and I wish to extend our profound gratitude to Mary and David Ostroff, owners of the Vacation Exchange Club in Youngtown, Arizona. Both have given generously of their time to not only clarify various points of exchanging homes and how their business operates, but to pamper us when we visited them in New York City and Youngtown.

I have aimed a stream of questions over the telephone and by letter to the owners of many other home exchange agencies, and I am grateful for their time and assistance.

Various sources contributed their time and assistance to make the Country Appendix complete. Noteworthy among these were foreign embassies and consulates based in the United States.

The "Advice Alerts" that appear throughout the text were written by experienced exchangers who took the time to respond to questionnaires I sent them. Thank you. One of these was the source of the ingenious currency exchange advice in chapter 8.

Finally, a sincere thank you to Sally Hill MacMillan, Director of The East Woods Press, for believing that a book written about a subject based as much on goodwill as it is on economy can be successfully marketed, and Editor Judy Patterson Pierson, who corrected my errors and became excited about home exchanging at the same time.

Table of Contents

Chapter 1 **What Is Home Exchanging?** 13
    A Definition
    Maximum Pleasure .... Minimum Cost
    Rio, Hong Kong, Sydney, San Francisco:
      No Problem
    The Cultural Connection
    Obscure Places And Off-Seasons
    What Home Exchanging Is Not
    Do You Have What It Takes?

Chapter 2 **The Existing Framework** 27
    Modern Home Exchange Agencies
    How The Agencies Work
    Does Supply Equal Demand?
    Educational Connections

Chapter 3 **Steps To Exchanging** 37
    Decisions, Decisions
    Target Your Audiences
    Getting The Word Out: Sources

Chapter 4 **Exchange Agency Catalogs** 47
    When Using An Agency Is A Good Idea
    The Catalogs
    Listing Yourself
    The Initial Contact
    The More You Advertise, The More Inquiries You'll Get

Chapter 5   Alternative Advertising 61
             Do You Need A Different Audience?
             Newspapers And Magazines
             Universities And Schools
             Community Host And International Visitor Services

Chapter 6   Making An Offer They Can't Refuse 73
             Home Packets
             Appraisals And Credit Ratings
             Questions To Ask Exchangers
             Working With An Interpreter
             Do It Quick

Chapter 7   The Five Thousand Mile Handshake 85
             Risk-Taking
             Comparing Potential Partners
             Rating Your Options
             Compensating The Deal
             Teachers, Students, And Other Long-Term Stays
             Written Agreements

Chapter 8   Easing Your Pre-Swap Worries 101
             Preparing To Trade Is Unique
             Insurance, Money, And Automobiles
             Yard Work, Bills, Deliveries, And Pets
             How To Make Life Easier For Your Partner And Yourself

Chapter 9   Enjoying Your Exchange 111
             Caring For Your Partner's Home
             Hospitality Exchanging
             Searching Out Those Local Favorites

Author's Note 117

Appendix A: General Information **119**
(The following listing contains organization title, address, and a description of services offered)

Home Exchange Agencies
Government Services And Educational Organizations
    Offering Home Or Hospitality Exchanges
Other Exchange Organizations
Reference Sources For Exchangers
Translation Services

Appendix B: Countries **139**
(The following listing includes schools, colleges and universities, major newspapers worldwide, and community host organizations by country)

Algeria	140, 157	Israel	146, 164	Sweden	150, 169
Australia	140, 157	Italy	146, 164	Switzerland	150, 169
Austria	158	Japan	146, 164	Trinidad and Tobago	150, 169
Bahamas	141, 158	Jordan	146, 164	Turkey	150, 170
Barbados	141, 158	Kuwait	146, 164	Uganda	151, 170
Belgium	141, 158	Luxembourg	165	United States	151, 170, 177
Bolivia	141, 158	Madagascar	165	Virgin Islands	176
Brazil	141, 159	Malaysia	147, 165	Wales	155
Canada	142, 159	Mexico	147, 165	West Germany	155, 176
Costa Rica	142, 159	Morocco	147, 166	Yugoslavia	155, 176
Cyprus	143, 160	Netherlands	147, 166		
Czechoslovakia	143, 160	New Zealand	166		
Denmark	143, 160	Norway	148, 166		
Egypt	143, 160, 177	Pakistan	148, 167		
England	144, 162	Panama	148, 167		
Finland	144, 162	Peru	148, 167		
France	144, 162	Philippines	148, 167		
Greece	144, 162	Portugal	149, 167		
Guatemala	145, 162	Puerto Rico	149, 167		
Guyana	145, 163	Saudi Arabia	149, 167		
Iceland	145, 163	Scotland	149, 168		
India	145, 163	South Africa	149, 168		
Indonesia	145, 163	South Korea	150, 168		
Ireland	146, 163	Spain	150, 169		

Appendix C: Home And Area Information List **185**

Chapter 1

What Is Home Exchanging?

We live in a wonderful world that is full of beauty, charm, and adventure. There is no end to the adventures that we can have if only we see them with our eyes open.

Jawaharlal Nehru

The traveler sees what he sees, the tourist sees what he has come to see.

Gilbert K. Chesterton

Most of the people I talk with have heard of home exchanging, yet many voice reservations about actually doing it. Assuming that you are somewhat skeptical yourself, this chapter is written with two purposes, to inform and to persuade. I want to explain the practice of home exchange, and then convince you that if you decide to, you can successfully exchange your home. One warning, though: Once you try it, you may be hooked.

A Definition

"Home exchanging," "house swapping," and "residence exchanging" all refer to the practice of trading homes for a designated period of time. Houses, duplexes, apartments, bungalows, cabins, even single bedrooms can be exchanged, in trades involving one, two, or more parties. Usually no money changes hands. Exchanges might only last one weekend or the agreement may cover a full year — it all depends on why the parties are swapping.

There are several distinct arrangements for exchanging. The most common involves a family from one area trading houses with a family from another area. This is a standard *single exchange*.

A *double exchange* involves two families in one area swapping with two families from another area. This arrangement doesn't involve any more planning time since each exchanger works on his individual arrangements. Participants cooperate just as if it were a normal exchange, but exchangers enjoy the advantage of having old friends with them in a new environment.

A *multiple exchange* is a more complicated, "circular" trade. A family in Palermo, Sicily, may travel to Vatican City, Italy to stay in an exchange family's home. The Vatican City family has simultaneously traveled to Nice, France, while the Nice exchangers have traveled by ferry to Palermo, thus completing the circle. This way you can establish connections and friendships with two exchangers rather than just one at a time.

A *moving multiple exchange* is similar to a multiple exchange, except that each family stays only a designated length of time at the exchange home and then moves to the next home in the circular exchange. Participating exchangers have nearly as much fun making the circular system work as they do vacationing. Disadvantages are increased travel costs and a great deal of planning time.

A *group exchange* involves a large group of people from one area swapping with another group from a different locale. Since group activities require extensive organization, group exchanges are usually facilitated by a mediatory joint concern, such as the International Center for Social Gerontology in the United States, which organizes exchanges between low-income elderly people. These exchanges, often underwritten by local merchants, emphasize education and cultural differences — the same values emphasized in a typical single exchange.

In a *hospitality exchange*, a family or single traveler stays with another family, agreeing to return the favor. For example, a family in Bonn, West Germany may reach tentative agreement to exchange with a couple in Luxembourg, but they are not able to arrange a mutually convenient date. The couple from Luxembourg, then, will come live with the Bonn family without charge, in exchange for allowing the Bonn family to come stay in Luxembourg when it's convenient for the Bonn family to do so. In a hospitality swap exchangers get to know each other very well, with the hosts serving as ready sources of advice to the visiting family. Arrangements are minimal; but space and privacy can be problems. Just as exchangers can become fast friends, they also can strain their budding relationship.

A *youth hospitality exchange*, whether arranged as part of a formal foreign student program or not, involves teenagers or college students living at home who "trade bedrooms," enabling each to experience living in a new family and culture, besides attending a foreign school.

In addition to these arrangements in which no money is paid to either participant is another option, *paid hospitality*. Providing hospitality to a paying single guest, family, or student for a nominal charge without a reciprocal visit is increasing in popularity. Paid hospitality is really the same thing as "bed and breakfast," but stays are typically longer.

Exchanges not involving payment are generally preferred since people are much more conscious of their behavior in someone else's home when they are invited guests, not paying customers. Paying guests often feel justified in taking certain liberties they otherwise wouldn't think of doing. Also, paying or accepting money can complicate both home and automobile insurance coverage.

You may have exchanged before without realizing it. Consider the following scenario: I'm on the telephone with a friend of mine who lives near Oakland, California. He wants to know if he can spend a couple of nights at my apartment the next weekend, since he'll be in town attending a sales seminar. "Sure," I say, "Oh, wait a minute. I have to be in the Bay Area those days. I was kind of thinking of dropping in on you!" The solution? Leave keys with the neighbors and trade places. That's home exchange, informal style.

Many kinds of people swap homes. Even though most exchanges involve two-child middle and upper-middle class families, there are many exceptions. I've heard of five members of a rock band annually trading their Seattle practice home with a retired couple from Los Angeles. The retirees enjoy taking camping vacations in the Pacific Northwest and having a house to periodically refresh in, and the rock musicians can't afford to rent a house in Los Angeles while they pursue record producers with their songs. I've talked with a young woman who traded a room in her parent's Lincoln, Nebraska home with a room from a young man in New York City. She wanted a modeling career and he had a scholarship to attend the University of Nebraska. Exchanging second homes or vacation homes is another alternative. What do these examples prove? Different people do have different needs, and a home exchange, when matched properly, is a very good way of satisfying both parties, at times irrespective of geography, income, or age.

Home exchanging, when first mentioned, usually receives quizzical, perplexed stares. Here's some of the common inquiries I receive.

"How does home exchanging differ from time-sharing?"

Time-sharing involves long-term commitments and financial investments of up to twenty thousand dollars, plus annual maintenance fees. In time-sharing you own the same time period year after year. In a home exchange, you're living in someone's home while they live in yours — there's no financial investment and no fees.

"Don't you feel strange living in someone else's home?"

No, not really. Most swaps don't happen overnight; you might have been thinking about your exchange for months. Through correspondence, you've become familiar with your partner's home, seen photographs of the premises, and have been left instructions for finding things and using appliances. All in all, upon arrival you're already quite "at home."

"Is it safe to leave your home to strangers?"

Again, you're not total strangers. Each of you through phone calls and letters have built up a moral obligation to the other. And, of course, *you* are in *their* home. This thought, in each partner's mind, is almost always enough to keep both parties honest. Besides, isn't it safer to have guests taking care of your home than to leave your house vacant and unprotected for several weeks? Following chapters explain how to draw up mutual contracts covering property damage or loss.

"Does it really work?"

Yes, it does. Thousands of people from all over the world swap every year. More than 60 percent of exchange agency subscribers resubscribe at some time. One couple from Mexico has exchanged over 60 times in just three years!

"Isn't it time-consuming and difficult to find a good match?"

The process does take time, but once you find several interested parties, it's just a matter of systematic mailings and, finally, deciding. A major criteria for finding the "ideal" trader is your mutual time and plan flexibility.

"Aren't disturbing surprises common?"

Surprises are very common. Disturbances are not.

ADVICE ALERT
(from Alan & Judy Kahn, New York City)
"TREAT THE EXPERIENCE AS AN ADVENTURE. ARRANGE IT SO THAT YOUR FRIENDS, RELATIVES, OFFICE WORKERS, ETC. INVITE YOUR EXCHANGEES TO THEIR HOMES FOR DINNER...THIS MAKES THE EXCHANGE VERY SPECIAL. TRY TO MAKE YOUR EXCHANGE EASIER BY USING LOCAL HELP (ARRANGED IN ADVANCE), E.G., CLEANING HELP, BABY-SITTERS."

Maximum Pleasure ... Minimum Cost

According to the Vacation Exchange Club in Youngtown, Arizona, over ten thousand homeowners annually trade houses, an estimate that doesn't include renters, apartment swappers, or those making their own contacts. And every year the number grows. Why?

Think of it this way. You won't be insulted any longer with cramped, impersonal hotel rooms; there won't be any maids, desk clerks, or waitresses to deal with, and there are no early checkout times. Regardless of the reason for your trip, whether it's to collect seashells, teach university students, or party in the Big City, by staying in a private residence you control the agenda. You decide if and when you dress up and jump into the fast-paced hotel-restaurant lifestyle. It's comforting to know that you can come back to the house, flick on the stereo, mix your own drink, and unwind. In private.

A bonus to staying in a home is that your new neighbors have lived in the area on a daily basis and can give you advice on what to do and what to see. Ask *them* about a good Chinese restaurant or the quickest route to the campus. They'll know from experience. Hotel guests, on the other hand, may be directed to restaurants, theatres, and other entertainments which are buying that hotel's endorsement. Even if you're staying in an unbiased hotel, who will be advising you? Either vacationers who are getting their tips out of a sight-seeing booklet will be making recommendations or the young desk clerk whose idea of a good time may differ ever so slightly from yours.

Residents tend to avoid local tourist attractions and instead spend their free time at favorite, out-of-the-way places they've found to be more enjoyable. For example, whenever my wife and I can't resist the lure of a short vacation, we usually find ourselves bicycling along the American River or wandering barefoot on northern California's beaches — familiar to us, but not to tourists. Your exchange neighbors might introduce you to their special spots.

Even though many people can't afford a luxury like a vacation in the popular sense, they can afford the transportation. The 1980s are a bargain hunter's delight for transportation.

Deregulation of the U.S. airline industry has meant that transportation fares haven't kept up with the rate of inflation. Who in the '70s would have foreseen $350 round trip New York to London fares, $500 Los Angeles to Tokyo prices, or $95 one-way fares from San Francisco to Honolulu? Add to that the discount rail passes now commonly available in Australia, Belgium, Britain, France, and over thirty other countries.

In what seems a curious contrast (and a very satisfying one to the exchanger), accommodation rates at hotels, resorts, and condominiums have risen rapidly in the U.S. since 1975. A room at Miami Beach which might have cost $45 a night in 1980 now rents for $85. A room at a not particularly plush New York City airport hotel costs over $100. Nicer hotels routinely charge from $200 to $300 a night. And you probably know from experience that restaurant tabs have kept up with accommodation expenses, price hike for price hike. A family of four can easily spend $200 a day just to sleep and eat, prior to any recreation or entertainment fees. Home exchangers, by taking advantage of inexpensive transportation fares and eliminating room rentals and constant restaurant tabs, are able to spend money on the tangibles that make trips memorable, if they choose to spend at all.

Rio, Hong Kong, Sydney, San Francisco: No Problem

You may be surprised to learn how many people would like to exchange homes with you. The secret to finding out who those people are and the breadth of your options is information — utilizing the advertising avenues available to you, and appealing to persons who would have a reason for wanting to cme to your locality. Cities are the natural place for most trades to happen, but the countryside is also fair game. Take a look at these example trades:

Ron, an Oregon botanist, was offered the chance to use the facilities at a marine science lab in the Florida Keys. Unfortunately, he would have to make his own accommodation arrangements. After trying unsuccessfully to find a Florida scientist who would rent him a room during his three-week stay, he did find a couple in an exchange directory with a four-bedroom house in the Keys. They agreed to a swap. "I couldn't figure out why they wanted to come to central Oregon," mused Ron, "but it turned out they were both raised here, and they wanted to visit relatives."

Jere and Rae Ann, along with their four children, traded their northern California home for an English family's Lancashire country castle for 24 days. "We paid under $3,000 for the whole trip, which wasn't bad considering air fare for all of us," said Rae Ann. "With kids, exchanging is really convenient. I'd just drive to the market for groceries. That and gas were our only real expenses in England."

Former neighbors John and Linda, avid scuba divers for many years, have long dreamt of exploring Australia's Great Barrier Reef, but the air fare, coupled with rooms, food, scuba and boat fees were always enough to scare them away. After contacting a family in Townsville, Queensland, however, their dream suddenly looked plausible. The Aussies had always wanted to visit the U.S., and not only were they willing to exchange their house and car, they also had a fishing boat. By using the craft as a dive boat "we saved a fortune," said John. "Those commercial boats charge over $100 a day per diver." Their total expenditure was $2,400 for three months of diving, with plane tickets and all expenses included.

Francoise, a professor, traded her Reims, France home for a three-week stay in Great Britain before spending another two weeks in

Limerick, Ireland. Both of Francoise's exchanges were with other teachers. "I had exchanged the year prior," she said, "but this one (a moving exchange) proved more exciting."

Usually both partners in an exchange trade for the same reason, to vacation. Other times parties in a trade may have identical objectives (securing the swap) but differing reasons for doing so. One partner may be attending a two-week workshop on astrology, while the other partner merely wants to get away from his job and surroundings. Because motives for exchanges can vary widely, the probability that you'll be able to make a trade desirable to you is good.

ADVISE ALERT
(from John W. Morris, M.D., Ormond Beach, Florida)
"HAVE LOTS OF COMMUNICATION. THE KIDS SHOULD BECOME PEN PALS AND THE WIVES, PARTICULARLY, SHOULD WRITE AND TALK TOGETHER ON THE PHONE TO FIND OUT WHAT EACH WILL NEED. BE ABSOLUTELY CANDID ABOUT WHAT YOU WANT. NOT DEMANDING, JUST HONEST. IT MIGHT BE SURPRISINGLY EASY TO GET."

The Cultural Connection

I've mentioned a few examples of exchangers able to save hundreds, even thousands of dollars off their usual vacationing bills. Money is the obvious, definable benefit of exchanging residences that attracts more beginners every year; but the ultimate benefit, the derivative that isn't so easy to impress on newcomers, is the exposure to authentic culture and the people you meet. This is why experienced swappers keep exchanging year after year.

Some people prefer to leave the details — indeed even the highlights — of their vacation to others. It's fine to visit Ireland, kiss the Blarney Stone, and watch crystal craftsmen at work in Waterford as participants of tour packages do. However, tour buses rarely allow for meandering along narrow downtown streets crowded with freckled fair-skinned Irish and slipping leisurely in and out of shops, even getting acquainted with some shop owners. These local citizens are your key to unlocking the mysteries about the countries you'll visit.

A tour guide or hotel clerk may well have an interest in *not* explaining political, racial, and economic issues gripping their country. But an acquaintance on a city bus or a neighbor living next door will be much more inclined to reveal issues honestly and without apprehension. By exchanging homes you can break through the facade erected by the tourism industry and enter the inside life of a community.

In exchange agency catalogs most of the advertisements you'll see are for primary residences. Still, according to the Vacation Exchange Club in the U.S., one-fourth of their listings are for second homes. Culturally, most vacation homes tend to be void of character. They're sterile. Here's a hypothetical example of how this can create problems. A couple advertises their vacation condo located at the famous ski resort, Sun Valley, Idaho. The condo is brand new, so new in fact that many of the other units built around it are still unsold. The couple bought the condo already furnished, and they are not including an automobile in the exchange offer since the condo is within quick walking distance of restaurants, ski lifts, shops, and all other facilities.

On the surface there is nothing wrong with this exchange offer. If the swap partners that our couple eventually match up with only want to ski to their heart's content they'll have a wonderful time. But if these exchangers come to the United States expecting to sample rural Americana, they might be sorely disappointed. The interior will be new but not intriguing, there may not be any neighbors to meet, and the people they do manage to meet may be from New York or California, not Idaho. If you're going to advertise your own second home, make it clear to interested exchangers what the home is like so that you'll find the right people.

Obscure Places and Off-Seasons

Brian and Julia, from their split-level home in Edinburgh, Scotland, mailed off letters of interest to eastern United States exchangers listed in an agency catalog. They sent 24 letters to people in New York City and, on a last irresistible impulse, mailed one letter to a lone exchanger in Norfolk, Virginia, who offered over 20 acres and a private estate. They wound up in Norfolk.

"We really didn't consider going to Norfolk because we hadn't heard of it," said Julia, "but he only received four offers and had a lovely home." Most of the New Yorkers received many offers, and only offered modest homes or apartments.

What does this mean? Just that you can get a far more tempting accommodation in out-of-the-way areas than in big cities. Here's another example. Mr. and Mrs. Harrison and their two daughters, tired of the Pacific Northwest chill, wanted to exchange their Vancouver, British Columbia house for a residence in Sacramento, California, to enjoy a warm spring holiday. They placed an advertisement in the *Sacramento Bee* newspaper and subsequently received several good offers within Sacramento County. Then they got a phone call from a woman in Woodland, a small town about 30 miles from Sacramento. She and her family lived on a fruit orchard and could offer horseback riding and fishing in addition to a large home with a pool and three cars, not to mention warm, sunny weather. The Harrisons chose Woodland.

Homes outside of big cities usually share the following five characteristics:

1. *The atmosphere will more accurately reflect the authentic local culture.* City apartments and houses have distinctive characteristics, but the people living in population centers reflect a cross section of society. It can be difficult to distinguish Tokyo from London from Los Angeles.

2. *They have relatively few tourist attractions.* Tourists tend to congregate in big cities, since so much happens there. This means that by exchanging to a less populated area you won't have to fight tourist congestion or pay tourism-inflated prices for food, entertainment, or transportation.

3. *The homes are usually larger.* A larger house can be particularly important if you have children with you. Many city homes are flats or apartments and were not constructed with children in mind.

4. *The network of neighbors is more solidly established.* In the city neighbors live very close together, yet often do not know each other. Out of the city a smaller population makes it easier to get to know people. To an exchanger like you, this means you're not just another anonymous face.

5. *There is more time to relax.* You may not want to relax on your vacation, but if relaxation is something you're looking forward to, a home in the country may be just the ticket.

Exchanges are not restricted to any particular season. Many people — especially retirees — are interested in making off-season trades. I've exchanged hospitality with a friend in Manhattan for a winter week. Why did I want to brave icy New York? Because I had business with certain publishers and that's where they're located. Do you think people from, say, Rhode Island, New Jersey, and Massachusetts would like to spend January in Arizona, New Mexico, or Nevada? It's quite possible. They could thaw in warm weather while the westerners might jump at the chance to see the historic Northeast. Some attractions are best viewed or exclusively offered in off-seasons. I know one woman who lives alone in a tropical country home from spring through fall but then in winter, when it's nicest, she swaps with another woman in a large U.S. metropolitan area where it's frosty cold. She leaves winter's warmth because she's a devout symphony goer, and the city philharmonic schedules its concerts during cooler months.

Undeniably most areas have a season which people prefer. Summer is always the most popular vacationing season, especially in Europe where "summer holidays" seem like an affliction. If you advertise in the right markets, however, you'll connect with others who also have a need for an off-season trade.

What Home Exchanging Is Not

The process of exchanging can seem deceptively simple. In fact, there is a substantial degree of responsibility that exchangers must accept in order to make the process work as well as it can. Unless exchangers act in mutually responsible and considerate fashion, one or both parties can get hurt.

Saving money can't be your only reason for wanting to exchange, and shouldn't be your primary reason, either. Learning a new way of life and allowing someone else to learn how you live is the proper emphasis. If you care about the quality of your experience, then you also will care about the quality of your partner's experience. The money savings is a bonus.

Home exchanging is not a spur of the moment travel idea for the unprepared. Experienced swappers can arrange a deal quickly, but only because they've learned how to provide for their exchange partners. And even then it takes time. People coming to your house from a foreign country especially require careful preparation on your part.

Without a doubt one of the most rewarding aspects of exchanging are the people you meet — especially your exchange partners. They may be close friends of yours for years to come. Some families look at exchanging as an investment in their children's future, a way of establishing a network of friends throughout the world that their kids can then stay with later on. The bond can become very strong. Of course, there is no commitment on behalf of the partners, but such enduring friendships as a result of exchanges are not atypical.

Once you're on the plane, this doesn't become a totally carefree type of holiday. As an exchanger, you assume responsibility for your partner's home. Even if you don't have to mow the lawn and feed the cat, you still have to look after the premises and leave it in the condition it was upon your arrival. Thoughtful exchangers try to leave a partner's home in *better* condition, hoping for reciprocal treatment. And who knows, you may want to return to the same house later on another exchange. A thank you card accompanied by a bottle of champagne and a vase of fresh flowers will leave the right impression and foster good will. And you never know, they might have done the same for you.

This isn't a "see everything, do everything" kind of vacation. You *can* exchange for a house and auto in London, and proceed to travel to Wales, Scotland, and Holland, but this much traveling erases much of the uniqueness of exchanging. Not only would you be hard put to care for your partner's home, you wouldn't get to establish friendships with your partner's neighbors nor really understand the daily pattern of life in London. You also would be sacrificing the economic advantages of exchanging since you'll be staying in hotels and eating out. Save the extensive sight-seeing for another trip, or do it prior to or immediately following your exchange.

Do You Have What It Takes?

Naturally you must have a place to offer for exchange. You also need something else: the will to do it. Here are ten traits that can serve you well:

1. *A desire to do the unconventional.* Be prepared for stares, dropped jaws, and questions galore when you tell your friends what you're planning to do.
2. *A positive attitude.* You can if you think you can. Believe that you, just like thousands of others, can exchange homes and come away delighted with the results.
3. *An ability to plan.* By flipping through this book's table of contents you can quickly see the emphasis placed on planning and preparing.

4. *A sense of adventure.* You must have the common sense to limit personal risk, and a willingness to gamble a little.
5. *Decision-making ability.* Choosing the best partner is made by relying on a balance of tangible proof and intuition.
6. *An open, objective mind.* Misunderstandings will occur. Maybe you won't be able to find the home computer operating instructions or the car will need an unexpected tune-up. At times like these you'll need patience to work differences out.
7. *An inquisitive nature.* Home exchanges are an education. Don't be satisfied to learn about other people and places from a television.
8. *Faith in others.* A trusting personality is a necessity. Because of the close relationship partners usually develop, your faith in others is rewarded with understanding and friendship.
9. *Consideration for your partner.* They may not speak your language or understand your society. Help them! It is a home exchanger's duty to do everything possible to ease the transition to a new home for one's partner — and to take care of the partner's home.
10. *A vivid imagination.* Think of the possibilities. A romantic second honeymoon in the Virgin Islands, a way to afford taking the kids to Europe, a chance to shop Singapore. In a very real sense your opportunities as a home exchanger are limited only by your imagination. Who would want to stay in your home? How can you reach them?

Chapter 2

The Existing Framework

The key that unlocks your first home exchange vacation is finding a suitable exchange partner. A suitable partner is above all someone living in an area you want to visit and who is willing to exchange with you. How do you find and contact such a person?

Someday the means by which interested exchangers contact each other may be rather centralized. Business people needing to visit an area for a prolonged period, teachers on sabbatical, students studying abroad, and vacationers all may be able to list themselves over an interconnected computer network that would instantly put parties in touch with one another, according to their needs and desires. For now, such a complete exchange infrastructure doesn't exist. What does exist is a number of small, privately-operated exchange agencies (some of which are joined together in loose confederations) and informal and often unpublicized governmental and educational services. Supplementing these disparate agencies and services is general and specific advertising that you can utilize, such as magazines, newspapers, school department faculty and public nonprofit organizations.

Modern Home Exchange Agencies

Private exchange agencies are very curious, intriguing businesses. No one knows for sure how many there are because the niches they carve for themselves can be quite small. Perhaps there are around 50 in the world that do nothing but offer home exchanges. If home rental agencies that will handle an exchange are included, the number may climb to several hundred (there's more money in rental commissions).

Some home exchange agencies do nothing but offer home exchanges. These agencies are what we'll concentrate on. To mingle exchange offerings with homes for sale or rent threatens the sanctity of the process and indicates that the agency owner strictly may be trying to make money out of the deal. Home exchanging, due to its history, is special. Agencies by and large have been operated out of goodwill, not for money. Try as new agencies might to pry subscribers away from more established agencies that operate mostly out of love for the system, they haven't succeeded. And that is the reason why the successful agencies remain small and generally unprofitable: the benevolent agency operators who preserve the integrity of the process inadvertently impede its growth for fear of ruining a vacationing system that is precariously based on the faith and honesty of the participants. Rest assured they are not making a killing.

This is not to imply that there is no killing to be made. In fact there are three very large (relative to home exchange agencies) private, computer-based American exchange networks for the owners of time-shared properties, with several more in other countries. The largest in the world, Resort Condominiums International, collects information from resort property developers and their clients concerning when during the year time-share owners would like to exchange their vacation time slot at their property for a vacation at another time-share property in another location. It then arranges exchanges between owners, or provides the information to the owners for them to make their own arrangements. There's a catch, however. Property owners can only exchange through the network if their resort landlord belongs to Resort Condominiums International, which can be expensive. On the other end of the communication line, they can only hope to match up with others belonging to RCI. Thus home exchangers, unless they own a time-share property in a resort development, are for the most part excluded from using this network to find partners.

One of the other time-sharing exchange systems, Exchange Network, has broken down this barrier. Ostensibly for time-share property owners, this service will nevertheless list and match your property and available time period regardless of whether you are offering a time-share property or a primary residence. They require a $50 life time membership fee plus another fee each time you arrange a match ($45 if contact is made via their printed catalog; $65 if contact is made through their computer), but they claim to offer 25,000 listings (600 of which are multi-complex resort owners, so there are actually many more than 25,000 to choose from). Their annual catalog cost was $47.70 in 1985 with quarterly updates. If you decide to choose from the catalog you merely note the listings that interest you and call the Exchange Network's toll free telephone number to book an exchange; otherwise, you can skip the catalog and telephone the network and they'll find you an exchange in the area desired and during the specified time period. The Exchange Network reports an 85 percent satisfaction rate from customers.

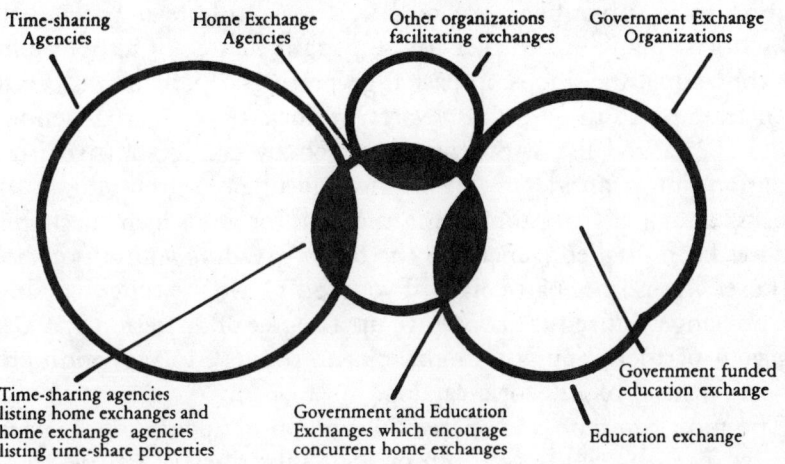

Relationships Among Home Exchange Agencies, Time-Share Agencies, Governmental, Educational, and Other Exchange Organizations

Will computer networks that blur the boundaries between time-share property exchanging and home exchanging wipe out the small home exchange agencies? Certainly the larger networks offer many more properties for exchange. The larger time-sharing networks do not, however, incorporate that most essential component of successful home exchange agencies, what I call the cultural component. Time-shared properties are nearly homogeneous in atmosphere. Their modernity and sterility impart a blandness in character. Time-shared properties are extremely functional but not too interesting, particularly for exchanges of extended duration. The agencies operated exclusively for primary home exchanges will retain their market and most likely become solidified with their constituencies — those wanting more than a resort vacation. The accompanying graph attempts to depict the relationship not only between time-sharing networks and home exchange agencies, but also the relative sizes and other organizations that advocate the process of exchanging homes.

Even though these private businesses and governmental and public organizations overlap in providing for home exchange and could benefit from sharing information, in most cases operators and owners are unaware that "circles" outside of their own circle even exist. Moreover, they are usually unaware of the participating businesses within their own circle.

How the Agencies Work

The basic function of the agencies is very simple. They collect information from subscribers, organize it, and distribute it back to the subscribers. Many of the agencies stop right there. All responsibility for contacting and choosing exchange partners is left to you. Other agencies provide more extensive services for a price, such as sending you a specialized list of potential partners by taking your particular situation into consideration, offering insurance, arranging credit checks, or actually consummating the deal for you. Such specialized services keep smaller agencies in the black. Availing yourself of these extra services is fine, particularly if you don't have the time to arrange the exchange yourself, but you give up a degree of discretion in choosing your partner. You also might end up paying $150 for additional services instead of $20 for a catalog.

The most common and successful method of advertising by agencies has been by word-of-mouth of their subscribers. I believe this is because most people find the idea of vacationing rent-free incredulous to the point of requiring persuasion from trusted friends who have already interchanged homes. A simple advertisement gets their attention, but it isn't enough to result in a subscription most of the time.

One of the largest confederations of exchange agencies, INTERVAC International, began in 1953 as a way for teachers in the Netherlands and Switzerland to trade homes during summer holidays.

Soon the founders realized that by encouraging expansion but retaining exclusivity over use and interchange of listings they could cultivate a loyal clientele. In 1961 an organizer in Great Britain was found; West Germany followed in 1965. By 1969, teachers participating through INTERVAC totaled 856. Crude mimeographed pages were distributed to subscribing teachers. Since 1975 membership has been growing at approximately 20 percent a year, in part a result of advertising to non-teachers as well as educators. INTERVAC affiliates now operate in Austria, Belgium, Brazil, Denmark, Finland, France, Ireland, Israel, Italy, Luxembourg, Norway, Spain, Sweden, and the U.S., as well as the four earlier countries and a sprinkling of subscribers in Bangkok, Hong Kong, Singapore, Bali, Kenya, Portugal, Venezuela, Africa, Australia, Canada, the Bahamas, Jamaica, Puerto Rico, the West Indies, French Polynesia, Greece, Mexico, New Zealand, and Tahiti. Affiliate organizers each collect yearly fees and home and preference data from subscribers in their own countries. The information is then published in catalog form by INTERVAC and distributed back to subscribers.

In the 1960s the largest market, the United States, was still being overlooked by INTERVAC. The oversight was not accidental. There was a question as to whether American teachers should participate, and the founders were cautious about expanding the concept. This delay in finding a U.S. organizer was to cost INTERVAC a big affiliate.

In 1960 an alternative home exchange agency was incorporated in New York City for American teachers by David Ostroff, a high school teacher. By 1963 the agency, Vacation Exchange Club, was receiving too much publicity to limit subscribers to teachers. Ostroff could find no good reason to deny participation so membership began to multiply.

Publicity about the Vacation Exchange Club caught the attention of Jeanne Ryder, who was starting Home Interchange Ltd. in England. Ostroff approved her proposal to work together to enhance the listings each could offer their subscribers and in 1964 they published a joint directory. By 1971 another agency joined representing Australia and New Zealand. This confederation became The Directory Group, named after the handsome directory published for subscribers.

Meanwhile, INTERVAC had found an organizer in the U.S., but by 1975 he decided that he could not compete against the Vacation

Exchange Club and recommended that Ostroff become the United States INTERVAC affiliate. This idea intrigued Ostroff since he could not meet the demand of his American subscribers for European exchange partners. He formally proposed a merger of The Directory Group and INTERVAC to the INTERVAC organizers. They refused a merger but wanted to share with their subscribers the Vacation Exchange Club's extensive offerings. They also were impressed with Ostroff's computerization of his operation and the exchange book he was annually preparing and having printed for The Directory Group. In short, they wanted the American affiliate but not the competing English agency. INTERVAC decided to accept Ostroff and his wife Mary (who had taken over daily management of the U.S. agency) as a full-fledged affiliate but stipulated that INTERVAC must have exclusive use of Vacation Exchange Club listings. The Ostroffs balked, but ended up supplying both The Directory Group members and INTERVAC affiliates with U.S. listings. Then in 1984 INTERVAC again issued the Vacation Exchange Club an ultimatum to receive exclusive use of U.S. listings. The Ostroffs declined and are now solely members of the Directory Group Association, which has since expanded to include affiliate organizers in Canada, Denmark, France, Germany, Ireland, Italy, the Netherlands, South Africa, and Spain. Subscribers are listed also from the Bahamas, Bermuda, Czechoslovakia, Greece, Haiti, Hong Kong, Hungary, Kenya, Liechtenstein, Mexico, Morocco, Panama, Portugal, Puerto Rico, Singapore, Tunisia, Scotland, Wales, the Virgin Islands, the West Indies, Yugoslavia and Zimbabwe. The grand opportunity to merge the two confederations into one large network was lost.

The advantage of combining the two groups would be mainly to subscribers like you and me. Instead of paying for a catalog with 4,000 exchange offers, a book with 10,000 offers would be ours. Moreover, the Directory Group Association and INTERVAC each have different strengths. DGA, for example, has many more listings in the U.S., Germany, Italy and Spain, a slight edge in Great Britain, and representation in Canada, Australia, New Zealand, and South Africa which INTERVAC lacks. INTERVAC offers more listings in Austria, Denmark, France, Ireland, the Netherlands, Norway, Sweden, and Switzerland, and representation in Belgium, Finland, Luxembourg, and Brazil which DGA lacks. A merger would balance the offers that subscribers could choose from. The cost of an expanded catalog would probably go up only marginally to reflect little more than shipping and printing increases.

There are many agencies that are neither affiliated with the Directory Group Association nor INTERVAC International, but in all cases their offerings are considerably more limited. Nevertheless, depending on where you live and where you want to go, smaller agencies can be advantageous for you if their supply/demand ratio is in your favor. InterService Home Exchange, Inc., for example, publicizes that their agency has maintained a more favorable balance for Americans going to England and France (fewer Americans for you to compete against for English and French offers) than any other American agency over the last several years.

ADVICE ALERT
(from Lilly Courtney, Mexico)
"THE MOST IMPORTANT THING TO ME IN AN EXCHANGE IS THE WONDERFUL FEELING OF BELONGING TO A NEW PLACE."

Does Supply Equal Demand?

In 1970 Pan American World Airways began sponsoring the Vacation Exchange Club, not so much to sell airline tickets as to improve its public image as a creative, innovative carrier. The J. Walter Thompson Agency in New York City publicized the "unique home exchanging concept," and the orders poured in to VEC. One major problem doomed the relationship, however: new subscriptions came in bulk from metropolitan areas served by Pan Am, throwing the Vacation Exchange Club listings out of balance.

The salient point derived from the Pan Am-VEC venture was the vital importance of agencies maintaining a geographic balance in the listing they send to their subscribers; for if subscribers from Florida and New York receive only a listing of interested exchangers living in Florida and New York, there will be a lack of home exchange options. There will exist a demand to exchange with persons in Europe, Asia, South America, and the U.S. West Coast that the agency is not supplying. The maintenance of a supply and demand balance is an important long-range job for exchange agencies or they will lose subscribers as quickly as they recruit them.

ADVICE ALERT
(from Barbara Sullivan, Malibu, California

"IF THERE ARE CHILDREN IN EACH FAMILY, IT'S GREAT IF THEY'RE AROUND THE SAME AGE SO THEY HAVE TAPES, BOOKS, TOYS, BIKES, ETC. I'VE LABELED MY KITCHEN CABINETS AND LINEN CLOSET SO EVERYTHING IS IN THE RIGHT PLACE WHEN I RETURN. I'VE EXCHANGED THREE TIMES AND HAD NO PROBLEMS."

All exchange agencies suffer from these supply and demand inequalities. For example, INTERVAC as a group now has a hungry demand from European subscribers for exchanges with Americans because the new INTERVAC U.S. affiliate, International Home Exchange Service, has a smaller subscriber base than the former INTERVAC U.S. list supplier. This makes exchanges to the U.S. tough for foreign INTERVAC subscribers but foreign exchanges comparatively easy for International Home Exchange Service subscribers, particularly midwestern and eastern Americans since a disproportionate number of International Home Exchange Service members live in California. As another example, in 1983 the INTERVAC affiliate in the Netherlands had a supply of almost twice as many subscribers wanting an exchange as the INTERVAC demand from outside the Netherlands provided; thus it was difficult for Netherlands INTERVAC members to find a partner but easy for INTERVAC subscribers desiring to go to the Netherlands to find a partner.

Inequalities in supply and demand mean that you should analyze the strengths and weaknesses of individual agencies on the basis of where you want to travel prior to subscribing. If you live in the U.S. and want to exchange to England, find out approximately how many American listings an agency has compared to how many it offers from England. If American listings outnumber English listings ten to one, the odds will be against you finding a partner, though this also depends on what you have to offer.

You also should inquire as to the general composition of an agency's subscribers. INTERVAC agencies were for a long time open only to teachers; thus a large proportion of their membership is still educators. European agencies of the Directory Group Association concentrated their advertising efforts at professional people. The income disparity between educators and professional people has resulted in more European DGA subscribers being interested in transatlantic exchanges than European INTERVAC subscribers, who, taken as a whole, tend to vacation to other European countries because the travel is less expensive and they prefer to vacation in Europe.

If you are likely to be a victim of the supply and demand curve due to where you live and or where you want to go, you would do well to consider either supplementing or supplanting your contact efforts through an agency with some form of alternative advertising.

Educational Connections

A professor at the University of Pittsburgh was offered an educational leave of absence with pay from his department to teach two semesters at Texas A. & M. University. A corresponding professor from A. & M. would teach in his place at Pittsburgh. No home exchange was planned along with the position exchange. Both professors received a monthly housing stipend, but neither payment was sufficient to cover the full rental. Thus both departments and both teachers ended up paying for accommodations.

This isn't always the case, but home exchanges are clearly an afterthought in job exchanges. What can traveling instructors do to find a partner? First, check out possibilities with the organization sponsoring the trip. You can write or call the Faculty Exchange Center listed in appendix A and try researching home exchange agency catalogs or advertising directly in newspapers, as well as writing notices to colleges in the area whose faculty you think might be interested in exchanging. These efforts can be bolstered by writing community host organizations, usually comprised of culture-conscious citizens in the local community. These groups do not exist to serve vacationing home exchangers but often times they will help educators in need of a home exchange by printing your offer in their newsletter.

I know a scholar from Great Britain who was selected for a visiting professorship in Philadelphia. Having home exchanged before, he wrote a letter to a New York world affairs group whose goal is to promote international understanding. The group president mentioned the professor's desire to exchange homes at a monthly meeting and a member in attendance passed on the information to a neighbor who was planning to spend six months in England. It worked. This twisted grapevine is not unusual in the home exchange communication process.

"Community host organizations are really fine ways to find an exchange partner," one exchanger told me. "They're always a bit perplexed by the request, but they seem to have a solid middle-upper class membership appreciating cultural exchanges.''

Another most productive audience for teachers are students where they'll be in residence. The number of students on any given campus is approximately 20 times greater than the number of faculty; and graduate students often need to conduct research away from their home campus. All you have to do is sort out the serious, responsible students from those who would park their motorcycles on your living room carpet.

The Fulbright-Hays Teacher Exchange Program, administered by the United States Department of Education, is the best example of a governmental exchange program that tries to inform participating teachers of the benefits and requirements of also exchanging your home with your overseas partner. The program's goal is to promote mutual understanding among the people of the world through educational exchanges to date 50,000 American and 90,000 foreign students, teachers, and scholars have been chosen for study and research awards. The teacher exchange operates job swaps between the U.S. and Canada, Denmark, France, West Germany, Italy, Switzerland, and United Kingdom, and at times other countries. Fulbright teachers are sent a preparatory guide, *Your Year In*, which devotes ten pages to exchanging accommodations. Any arrangements and agreements are left entirely to the participants. If the pair of participants for some reason want to exchange homes but don't, they, of course, can attempt to find partners through other means.

Chapter 3

Steps To Exchanging

Contemplation, research, information, and coordination. These are the steps involved in exchanging. The amount of work involved depends on your own situation: where you want to go, how flexible your plans are, and what you have to offer for exchange. A gorgeous house in a popular area "sells" itself. If that's your situation you won't have much to research. Similarly, if you're amenable and a bit capricious, contemplation may consist of a barely considered "Okay!" But most of us will have to partake in at least a bit of salesmanship, and have definable destination preferences as well. Each of these four considerations — contemplation, research, information, and coordination — is an important facet in arranging your exchange.

Decisions, Decisions

It doesn't take a great deal of prodding to get people to fantasize about places they'd like to go. Many of us would jump at a chance to lie around on Maui, drink lager in Munich, or attend the opera in Milan. If your reason for exchanging is solely to vacation, then preferential destinations need only be tempered with data about the places in question and your personal finances.

If you're exchanging for educational or business reasons, however, your personal preferences are outweighed by need. A law professor at

Harvard University in Massachusetts may be asked to teach a semester at Calgary University in Canada. A California entomologist may receive a grant for research in Argentina. German production managers may be sent by their employers to observe labor-management relations in Japan. These situations dictate where the travelers will go; thus personal preferences may be of little or no importance.

Vacationers can use a set of criteria called "locale factors" to help them in deciding on primary exchange locations. Locale factors include currency exchange rates, energy prices for home heating and air conditioning, automobile gasoline prices, climate, season, and political stability. Use these factors to assist in rating potential destinations. Professors trading jobs and people on business may not be in a position to determine where they will exchange, so locale factors are not as useful to them.

If money is a concern, currency exchange rates should certainly be investigated. Most brokerage firms and major banks will quote you the latest currency rates. Ask them for toll-free numbers you can call. Between 1983 and 1985, for instance, the dollar was very strong, while the French franc was relatively weak, meaning that an American in Paris could purchase much more for his money than a French exchanger in New York City could buy. The French citizen would have been better off financially to exchange with someone in London or, better yet, Mexico City, since the pound and peso also were weak and postponed his U.S. trip until a more favorable dollar-franc exchange rate developed.

Rate of inflation is important if you will be exchanging for a lengthy period, say, six months or longer. The lower the inflation the better. You probably wouldn't notice a ten percent rate of inflation, but 100 percent annual inflation — now commonplace in less developed countries — might send you back home prematurely.

Utility rates vary widely. For example, electricity in Honolulu can cost four times more than the same usage throughout much of California.

Europeans traveling to the U.S. or Canada will be pleasantly surprised by the comparatively low prices for gasoline, whereas North Americans should plan on limited driving in Europe because of high gasoline prices and put a greater emphasis on riding mass transit.

Climate and season are naturally important considerations but not only for weather reasons. If you'll be exchanging to a popular tourist area, prices of everything from groceries to guided tours drop as much as 25 percent in the off-season. Attractions also will be much less crowded during off-season months.

If you'll be taking children along, consider areas with ample recreation facilities to keep them entertained. They might consider the pristine deserted island you chose a dungeon.

The political stability of each area is another factor in choosing a destination for home exchanging. A political science instructor or a writer may find Central America or the Mideast fascinating, but ruling out an area prone to violence won't necessarily dampen the vitality of your experience.

Initially you needn't pinpoint your possibilities to just one area. It is preferable to remain uncommitted to any particular area since flexibility in planning increases your chances for matching up. Narrowing your interests somewhat does help though, since nearly all the listings in an exchange agency catalog sound tempting, and you may be under time and financial constraints. It isn't too painful to eliminate Canada and Brazil from consideration, for example if you still have Sweden, Italy, and Greece to choose from.

Target Your Audiences

As stated, people the world over have various needs. Here's an example.

Raymond owns a small, two-bedroom home in a suburb of sprawling Los Angeles. Like everyone there, Raymond has a car, this one a Ford Pinto in need of a tune-up. Ray's mother, whom he hasn't seen in several years, moved to Detroit after Ray's father died. Now she's going to be remarried and wants Ray at the wedding, but her husband-to-be doesn't want 39-year-old Ray staying with them during their first romantic week together.

Curtis is a 24-year-old Detroit autoworker who has spent the last six years assembling Ford Pintos. That is, until he was recently laid off. Now he's trying to sell his modest brick house and move to Los Angeles. Since he wants to know how much to ask for his house and furniture, Curtis reads the classified ads in the *Detroit Free Press* every day.

Raymond does a bold and daring thing. He calls the *Free Press* long distance and places an ad with his phone number, offering his home for a Detroit home for one week. Curtis sees the ad, reasons that a rent-free week of job hunting would be worthwhile, and also does a bold and daring thing. He calls Ray. Raymond agrees to show Curtis' brick home to any interested callers while he's staying there, and Curtis agrees to tune up Ray's sluggish Pinto. ***Cambio! Tauschen! Exchange!*** Some exchangers will be more interested in your offer than other exchangers. Lisa, a successful insurance saleswoman in Detroit, also may have seen Ray's ad, but had a three-week vacation coming up, not one week. Henry, whose company built Ray's Pinto, saw the ad but didn't bother calling since Ray didn't mention having access to a pool. Monique, a French doctor renting an apartment in Detroit, wanted to visit Los Angeles but didn't see Raymond's ad.

If Ray had listed his home and car in an exchange agency catalog he probably wouldn't have found a partner. He would have had to have known of his mother's wedding far in advance since directories are published two or three times a year. Ray's situation called for a different method of marketing, the results making it clear that you can reach different people by various means of advertising. Blindly advertising can result in poor offers or no offers, while wasting your money. The people most likely interested in exchanging with you should be identified. To do that requires a close examination of what you have to offer.

Here are some examples of homes and area attractions. After reading each description, try to think of good outlets to advertise their exchange availability:

1. A retired couple wants to exchange their three-bedroom home in Scottsdale, Arizona, for one month next spring with no preference of where to go. Included are a pool and car. The weather will be warm, and a number of major league baseball teams play exhibition games in Scottsdale during spring. How can they best make an exchange?

Suggestions: Since the couple will go virtually anywhere, listing their home in an exchange directory may work since they won't be excluding offers on the basis of location. Both weather and pool would appeal to vacationers. Approaching advertising from the baseball angle, however, is more specific and might yield quicker results. A phone call to a local newspaper or the front office of any major league team would reveal which teams would be in or near Scottsdale. Then our exchangers could advertise in the newspapers that circulate in those cities, hoping to lure some calls from die-hard fans.

2. A family of three wants to exchange their apartment in Honolulu for a home in Chicago. The mother is a research specialist in Hawaii and is invited to teach a semester at Northwestern University.

Suggestions: Since she is only interested in the Chicago vicinity, an exchange directory won't provide enough listings to justify buying the catalog (although some cities, like San Francisco and New York City, are represented with many listings). Honolulu is a popular vacation resort, so she would probably have great success through the *Chicago Sun-Times* or *Chicago Tribune* newspapers; however, since she needs to stay for three to four months, she might first try advertising to faculty and students at Northwestern, the University of Chicago, Columbia College, and Loyola University.

3. A 23-year-old graduate student lives with his family in Brest, France. He was born in Rochester, New York, and wants to return there for two or three weeks. What should he do?

Suggestions: He can buy an exchange directory and hope to find a Rochester exchanger offering a hospitality swap, but a better bet would be to contact the U.S. National Council for International Visitors, which lists community groups willing to help house international visitors during short stays. Rochester, for example, has three such services: the Rochester International Friendship Council, International Visitor Program Service, and a Rochester Association for the United Nations. He also might write the international centers at Rochester colleges to attempt to exchange bedrooms with a Rochester student who wants to visit France.

4. A farming family of five lives in a secluded house next to one of Ireland's blue ribbon fishing streams and wants to come to America. Although the countryside is beautiful, the family doesn't have an automobile to swap, so access to tourist attractions would be poor or expensive. How can this family hook up in an exchange?

Suggestions: The hopeful exchangers should play up the attributes of their immediate area, which could be the trout stream and the *lack* of access. Their best choice is to place a classified ad in U.S. magazines that cater to fishermen, such as *Angler, Arkansas Sportsman, Field and Stream,* or *Fly Fisherman Magazine.* These readers wouldn't care so much about the lack of an auto; they'd be thinking about fishing in Ireland in an out-of-the-way "hot spot."

This is what target your audiences means. Analyze your situation and list the things about it that would interest others. Then think of how to reach those particular audiences, whether they be the broad category of vacationers or relatively narrow categories such as baseball fans, fishermen, professors.

ADVICE ALERT
(from J.R.S., Steamboat Springs, Colorado)
"MEET THE PEOPLE YOU ARE EXCHANGING WITH AT BOTH ENDS OF YOUR TRIP, FIRST AT ONE FAMILY'S HOME, THEN THE OTHER'S, WITH YOUR VACATION TIMES SLIGHTLY OVERLAPPING. WE'VE OFTEN ENJOYED THEM AS MUCH AS THEIR HOMES."

Zeroing in on exact audiences who might have a need or strong desire to exchange with you enables you to "climb" up or down the international socio-economic ladder. Most people assume that a prerequisite of exchanging homes is that the trade be equivalent in terms of house value and area attractiveness, but this is a fallacy. Economic equality is not a prerequisite, honesty is. A wealthy account executive in Madrid may not care if he only gets a $40,000 rural house in exchange for his $250,000 penthouse. It's only temporary, and it may offer something refreshingly different. Swapping with an exchanger whose needs are markedly different from yours often results in perfectly cordial and satisfying yet economically unequal exchanges.

Getting The Word Out: Sources

Information. The whole process of trading homes is simply information until the actual switch takes place. Direct information sources useful to home exchangers are in the appendices of this book, so you are well-equipped to advertise your home. There are, however, a number of very useful reference books listed in appendix A that are not so specific, but still can assist in locating your target audiences. This means you'll be using your local library as a liaison to connect you with other exchangers, and a better liaison there is not. If you know how to use your library (or are on friendly terms with the librarian) the whole world will be yours to contact.

The sheer quantity of people you reach is terribly important. If you'll be sending notices to universities announcing your exchange availability, don't just send one notice to each school. The right people probably won't see it. Send 100 to each school! If you're going to mail out form letters to people listed in exchange directories, don't send five letters and sit around hoping for replies. Make things happen. Send 50! Ambitious advertising assures that you'll receive more offers, sooner.

Consternation is easy when trying to decide which advertising channels will produce the quickest, best results. How do you decide?

There is no general, systematic method for choosing a newspaper over a university, or a home exchange over a travel magazine. But by carefully considering your own situation, logical choices can point to an "effectiveness ranking" of the various information channels available to you. Following are three lists of advertising options in priority rankings for the groups *Teachers/Scholars, Students,* and *Vacationers/Businesspeople.* But these options don't have to be carried out one after the other. You can try all of them at once if you want fast results.

Sources of Finding a Partner for Teachers/Scholars
1. Your job exchange partner (if any)
2. Your sponsoring organization (if any)
3. School or institute faculty where you're going, along with other area schools
4. Community host organizations
5. Home exchange agency catalogs
6. Student bodies of area schools
7. Local newspaper and magazine classified advertisements
8. Word-of-mouth

Sources of Finding a Youth Hospitality Partner for Students
1. Your school exchange partner (if any)
2. Your sponsoring organization (if any)
3. Community host organizations
4. Your own school's International Center
5. Student bodies of schools in the area where you'll be going
6. Home exchange agency catalogs

Sources of Finding a Partner for Vacationers/Businesspeople
1. Home exchange agency catalogs
2. Local newspaper, local magazine, and regional or national magazines
3. School, university, and institute faculties
4. Professional organizations and clubs
5. Word-of-mouth
6. Community host organizations
7. Other

Teachers/Scholars. If you have a job exchange partner, that should be your first place to look when making a home exchange. After all, that person lives where you're going to live and will be away from home for the same period you'll be gone. Perhaps most important is the fact that even though you don't know this person yet as a friend, you know who he is and how to reach him.

If you don't have a job exchange partner or don't come to agreement with your job partner, write the organization sponsoring your exchange. Ask them to please check their files to find out whether any other teachers in the area you're going to also are exchanging to your school area.

Your third step in advertising your availability should be to send packets of notices to schools in the area you'll be living in, for direct distribution to the respective faculty. A fourth measure is to write a letter explaining your offer to any local community host or international visitor organizations in the area.

Home exchange agency catalogs can be of use since a great percentage of these members are teachers themselves with schedules similar to yours. Members usually don't desire a stay of over four months, although you could try to arrange for one exchanger to come for the first few months, and then have another come (but this means you'll be moving from place to place too). Exchange catalogs can be more useful to you if you live in a popular vacationing area and have a nice home. Also, your chances are much improved if you know of your school assignment far enough ahead of time to get an advertisement in the February catalogs, since timing is crucial in finding a partner.

If you have a choice of when to exchange jobs and can avoid committing yourself for awhile, your chances with an agency catalog will be better since some members may live in the right areas, but can only trade at certain times.

If the educational institution you will be working at has a substantial number of graduate students in particular, you should consider advertising to the student body. Graduate students are more mobile than undergraduates.

Daily and weekly newspapers are, of course, another advertising channel though it may prove more difficult to find someone willing to exchange for a long period of time.

Word-of-mouth information was ranked low not because it's ineffective — quite the opposite — but most people just don't have a broad network of friends who can help inquire of their friends about a home exchange. If you have the personal contacts, by all means use them.

Students. As with instructors, the first two sources to check are your school exchange partner and your sponsoring organization if you're swapping one to one with another student or if a group is sponsoring or arranging your trip. Many community host organizations and international student community groups can help with a hospitality exchange, though they are mostly geared toward helping students on short stays of a few days. Nevertheless, they'll try to help you if they have the time.

If you'll be going to a heavily populated area, check the home exchange agency catalogs for families advertising a willingness for a youth hospitality exchange. A more productive bet might be to write student newspapers in the area, requesting that they run a classified ad for you.

It isn't necessary or practical for students to seek a youth hospitality swap if they are traveling via a scholarship program that pays for their housing. A swap can still be a valuable cultural experience compared to living in a dormitory, but arranging a swap takes time and sincere commitment. If a swap won't save them money, most students would just as soon agree to prearranged, paid-for housing by their sponsor.

Vacationers/Businesspeople. For vacationers who live in a popular area and or have a nice home to swap, contacting exchangers through agency catalogs will pay off. Newspapers can work better for businesspeople who need to swap to a certain area at a particular time.

Many people exchange homes the first time with people they've met at parties, through mutual friends, or by both belonging to professional groups or clubs. Dentists swap with dentists, retired Air Force personnel with other Air Force retirees. Community host organizations will be reluctant to assist you in finding an exchange partner in their areas since they've been formed primarily to help educators, students, and prominent international governmental guests.

ADVICE ALERT
(from Louisa S. Cooper, Balboa Island, California)
" WIVES: DON'T WORRY ABOUT YOUR "THINGS." YOUR POSSESSIONS WILL PROBABLY BE CARED FOR BETTER THAN YOU CARE FOR THEM YOURSELF. BE PREPARED TO MAKE FRIENDS! YOU GET TO KNOW PEOPLE VERY WELL WHEN YOU TAKE THEIR PLACE IN THEIR OWN HOUSES."

Chapter 4

Exchange Agency Catalogs

One of the advantages of being disorderly is that one is constantly making exciting discoveries.

A.A. Milne

It can't be ignored that more individuals and families exchange homes each year through agencies than through any other method. Since agency services and catalogs are tailored for home exchangers, they have certain advantages over newspaper, magazine, and school advertisements.

When Using An Agency Is A Good Idea

Since nearly all agencies are geared toward vacationers and summer months are preferred for enjoying holidays, agency catalogs are seasonal in use. They are not evenly effective year-round. Catalogs are usually published and sent out to subscribers in January or February, with a supplement of late listings (ads placed by people who didn't return their order forms and payment in time to get in the first edition) being mailed out in April or May. This means that if you want to vacation sometime from May to September the catalogs will be well suited to your needs. And since exchangers try to line up partners early to insure they'll be spending their holidays somewhere other than their own backyards, you too must be prepared to act quickly. If you procrastinate, the better opportunities will be taken. That means you must be thinking ahead and mail in your advertisement early. If you miss the deadline for the main catalog and instead are listed in the supplement, your chances of finding a satisfactory partner decrease.

Agency organizers are sensitive to this problem and some go out of their way to help luckless and late exchangers find partners. Even after the first or second catalog supplement is sent out, some agencies still will circulate informal photocopied "late lists" to members or telephone affiliated agencies with last minute data on available exchangers. Still, using an agency makes far more sense if you are able to send in your application in time to advertise in the first, main catalog.

The Catalogs

Before joining an agency, ask yourself four questions. First, how many listings does the agency have? If you'll go more than one particular place, the sheer quantity of listings is a deciding factor. Secondly, how well balanced are their listings? If their advertisers are virtually all from your part of the country the odds that you'll find a partner outside your area through that agency are diminished. Thirdly, where are most of their listings? If you need to swap to Los Angeles but all of the agency's West Coast listings are in northern California, Oregon, and Washington, they're of no use to you. Lastly, how long has this agency been in business? The percentage of agencies that fold within two years is high, with stories of "agencies" closing as soon as the subscriber checks come in not unheard of. Join an established firm. One peek at a catalog, or a letter of inquiry can reveal the answers to all four questions.

Most agencies mail out photocopied or printed pages of subscribers with one or two paragraphs describing each listing. Since these agencies deal primarily with American, Canadian, British, and French exchangers, the language printed is invariably English. The INTERVAC affiliated agencies, to encourage more diverse international exchanges, developed a Trans-Lingual Abbreviation Code, which has been closely adopted by the Directory Group Association. Since the catalogs of these organizations are so widely distributed and the coded listings can look rather intimidating (though intriguing) to newcomers, I will briefly explain how to decipher the code.

Trans-Lingual Abbreviation Code

a c air conditioning	h f stereo/hi-fi	r o quiet neighborhood/peaceful surroundings
a e use of car/car exchange	h h domestic help available	r r den/family room/playroom
a g acreage/extensive grounds	h p facilities for handicapped	r t restaurants
a n car necessary	h s use of second home	s a sauna/hot tub/Jacuzzi
apl all appliances	h t hunting	sba swimming (private)
a q antiques	i interests	s c security/doorman
b b barbecue	i c infant-care facilities	s d scuba diving/surfing
b c deck/balcony/porch	j (followed by country abbreviation) and language preferred for correspondence	s e boating/sailing
b i use of bicycle(s)		s k skiing
b s baby-sitters available		s l sabbatical
c a use of motor home/caravan/trailer	l a lake	s p swimming (public)
c c country club privileges	l i elevator/lift	s s spectator sports
c f tourist attractions/resort area	m k modern kitchen	t convenient public transportation
c l cultural attractions	m o microwave oven	t e tennis
c s convenient shopping	m t mountains	t r theatre(s)
c u college/university	m u museum(s)	t v television
d k darkroom	n near	u b use of boat
d r clothes dryer	n c no children	u z view
e e experienced exchanger	n p no pets	w a hiking/walking
f i fishing	n s non-smokers only	w f waterfront
f n friendly neighbors	o ocean	w k workshop
f o forest/woods	p c pet(s)/exchange pet care	w m clothes washer
f p fireplace(s)	p i piano	w v dishwasher
g d garden	p k park/playground	y d terrace/patio/yard
g g garage/parking	p l beach	z sea
g o golf	p v seclusion/privacy	
g v unpolluted	r i horseback riding	(1978 Vacation Exchange Club)

This code is used both to save space and to facilitate better international understanding. Subscribers in each country receive a translation of the code key (pictured above) in their own language. These codes are then integrated into each listing as follows:

U, BOSTON, 3M, E   X,XH   4W, 31/7-27/8/86, F
Hideki Yoshida   2/0/0   B, 5, 3, 2   EUR, C
999 Mariposa De Oro, Boston 02108   (617 998-4342)   musician//
ac ae ag apl aw bc bs cc cf cl cu dr ee fn gd mk mu ns pl p-v ri rt sa tv wm wv z

---

Translated, this advertisement says that Hideki Yoshida, a musician living in an urban area three miles east of Boston (U, Boston, 3M, E) seeks either a home exchange or hospitality exchange (X,XH) for four weeks, July 31st to August 27, 1986, and this is the only time he can go (4W, 31/7-27/8/86, F). Two adults, no teenagers, and no children will exchange (2/0/0). The home is a multi-floor house (B) with room for five people in three bedrooms with two baths (5,3,2). Yoshida wants to exchange with people living in either Europe or Canada (EUR, C). His address is 999 Mariposa De Oro, Boston MA 02108, and his telephone number is 617 998-4342. The letters on the bottom two rows tell readers that Yoshida's house has air conditioning, he wants to exchange cars, and the home is on extensive acreage (ac ae ag). The house includes all appliances (apl) and the home is furnished with antiques, has a deck, balcony or porch, and baby-sitters are available (aq bc bs). You can enjoy country club privileges (cc) and tourist attractions (cf), cultural attractions (cl), and a college or university (cu) are all nearby.

The home has a clothes dryer, Yoshida is an experienced exchanger, and you'll have friendly neighbors (dr ee fn). The house has a garden (gd), modern kitchen (mk), museums are close by (mu), and he doesn't allow smoking in the house (ns). A beach (pl) is near, and the area is secluded (pv). You can ride horses (ri), too. There are restaurants in the area (rt), Yoshida has either a sauna, hot tub, or Jacuzzi (sa), there's a television set (tv), clothes washer (wm), dishwasher (wv), and the sea (z) is close by.

Here's another example from an exchanger in the Virgin Islands:

Z, CHARLOTTE AMALIE, 5M, NE   0   2M, 14/2-30/5/87, 0
Shad Curry   2/2/1   D, 3. 2, 2   0
Mira Loma Rd., St. Thomas 00801   (809 733-5050)   ret. Army//
warm water snorkeling
 se go te dr wm gg sc sba tv uz ro np fi
reply in English PHOTO

This one's from Shad Curry, who lives on the shore (z) of St. Thomas Island, five miles northeast of Charlotte Amalie. He's open to any kind of exchange offer (0) and would prefer two months between February 14 and May 30, 1987, though he is open to any duration or time you suggest (2M, 14/2-30/5/87, 0). Curry will be bringing another adult, two teenagers, and one child (2/2/1). He's offering a vacation home (D) which sleeps three in two bedrooms with two baths (3,2,2). He's willing to go anywhere (0). He lists warm water snorkeling, boating/sailing (se), golf (go), tennis (te), clothes dryer (dr), clothes washer (wm), a garage (gg), and security/doorman service (sc). Private swimming, television, and a nice view are included (sba tv uz), as is a quiet neighborhood (ro). No pets are allowed (np), fishing is nearby (fi), and Curry requests all correspondence in English. A photograph (PHOTO) of his home is included with his advertisement.

Since the code isn't used in the first two lines of each listing and these lines contain the most important information about each listing, the agencies have adopted pictographs, shown here, to assist in filling out subscription forms and browsing through the catalogs.

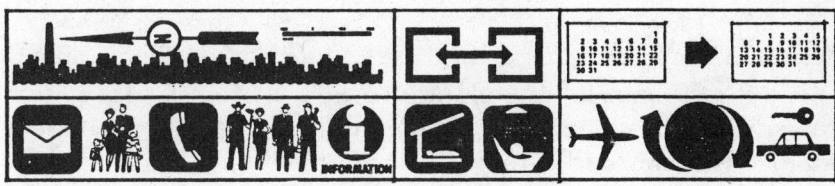

As you look through either the INTERVAC or DGA catalog, you only need to read the first two lines of each listing to decide whether the advertisement interests you or not. If so, decipher the abbreviation code. Most agencies don't use any code, instead preferring to print full word or abbreviated descriptions of offers. One agency that doesn't use any coding in its listings is InterService Home Exchange in Glen Echo, Maryland. Its listings look like this:

PARIS. Large house *en dupleix,* located in lively Les Halles section. 4 bdms 2 bths, cen htg, wshr/dryer, dshwshr, fridge, TV, car. Exchange only. (Name, address & telephone number here.) Marketing Research. 2 adult 3 child. Prefer 4 weeks end July-end Aug in USA (Los Angeles or between Boston & New York). Fr, Eng. Prefer House near ocean in above areas.

Note how listings such as this one cannot contain as much information as a coded entry, but this layout sure makes for easy reading when flipping through a catalog. The InterService Home Exchange catalog also contains some listings in French.

Here's another style of listing from Holiday Exchanges in Ventura, California:

Name & Address
OFFER
EXCH/RENT 3-BR 2-ba ranch style hse w/priv htd pool; panoram view of sea, mtns & desert; nr golf, tennis, fishing, SKIING, hunting, shopping, rstrnts; easy drive to culture ctrs, theaters, museums, rec area; one/half hr to Disneyland, Lion Safari, etc. Car avail for exchange.
REQUEST
Flexible, suggestions requested; anywhere, anytime. Reasonable RENTAL if exch not feasible.

Home to Home Holidays in the Netherlands assigns a code to each subscriber which is located in the front of their International Holiday Journal with preferred dates as well as in the listing, like this:

MOROCCO-714 CASABLANCA !!!
D,43b-wp; Lv:28sq m, radio, hifi; large balcony loggia; Gar.av; Vw:hous.w.gard.,park;Traff:1;8th.fl. grand standing comfort. apartm; no pets, no child. under 7; household. lady av. (without extra charg.); Seabeach, sw.pl:3; Centre:near

Holiday 80, based in Cork, Ireland, Simply lists addresses of interested exchangers by country along with their preferential destinations.

Listing Yourself

Before hastily scribbling out a check to an agency make sure they are in fact in the home exchange business. Some agencies may have been in the home rental business for 35 years and sound distinguished and well established, but only recently started to list home exchanges. They might not have many exchange listings yet.

ADVICE ALERT
From Barry & Margery Strom, Stamford, Connecticut:
"BE AGGRESSIVE! DON'T WAIT FOR SOMEONE TO CONTACT YOU; YOU'LL WAIT ALL YEAR. GO WITH YOUR GUT FEELING ABOUT THE PEOPLE. TRUST YOUR OWN REACTION TO THE EXCHANGE FAMILY. ONCE THE EXCHANGE HAS BEEN ARRANGED, BEGIN COLLECTING INTERESTING INFORMATION ABOUT YOUR AREA YOU CAN LEAVE FOR THE FAMILY. ORGANIZE A BOOK OF INTRODUCTION ON YOUR HOME, GOING ROOM BY ROOM, EXPLAINING THE SPECIAL WORKINGS OF YOUR HOME."

You might consider joining more than one agency. Catalogs are typically undervalued. When writing for subscription forms, ask for a rough breakdown of how many listings the agency has in each country. If you want to go to Finland and you're trying to decide between joining INTERVAC or DGA, the decision is easy since the Directory Group Association doesn't have any listings from Finland. In Italy the DGA has a lopsided advantage. But if you want to go to or swap within Great Britain, both groups have strong affiliates, as do some other American agencies. Why, for instance, only subscribe to DGA and get 850 Great Britain listings when you could also subscribe to INTERVAC and get 650 more? What's an extra $25 for access to a second agency's membership when the payoff may be a month-long vacation? Finding a partner is going to save you $40 to $100 in bed and breakfast fees per night. The catalogs— especially the larger ones and those with a balance of listings in your geographic favor — are a bargain.

Writing your advertisement for a catalog seems easy enough, but how your ad reads partially determines how many responses you'll receive. The ad is the only message about yourself that people will have. Take the time to write it carefully. The amount of creativity and writing skill needed depends on which agency you're joining. As you've partially seen, some print what you write, others rewrite your text, while some require that you write in code. But even with the dry, coded entries you can make people notice your ad.

Ideally, you have access to an old catalog from a friend or library reference room. By scanning listings it is easier to understand what attributes make one entry stand out over another. As a rule, list highlights about your area rather than your home. Vacationers usually use a home as a base from which to explore area attractions. Do you know anyone who goes to Hawaii to watch television? Attributes like "Sea Lion Caves, Crater Lake, Trees of Mystery" intrigue and inspire more so than "large deck, dishwasher, garage." Do people really care on first contact whether your home has a darkroom or barbecue? These things are nice to have, but they are only extras. Spend more of your allotted space describing tourist attractions or the surrounding area's natural beauty.

If you have a car that's efficient, racy, or especially comfortable, and you plan to exchange it, put that in the ad. Most people do swap autos but don't advertise the type or model. A desirable car is very important to many people. Europeans coming to the United States especially look forward to driving since fuel is comparatively inexpensive. If you've got a Mercedes, BMW, Porsche, or Cadillac convertible, by all means advertise it.

When you're given a limited amount of coded space and advised to abbreviate home and area features, consider using some whole words to highlight area attractions and draw reader attention. An ad reading "charming victorian twnhse gdn apl ac fp ro tr mu pk cf, walk to Met Museum, Lincoln Ctr," is infinitely more arousing than "mt fo la gv fn ag bb bc apl fp sba uz wf gd ac mk yd hf fi sk ht wa ns an np pk." Make them *want* to read your ad.

Paying extra to include a small photograph with your ad is a catch-22: if the photo turns out good when reproduced it can say more complimentary things about your home than the written copy, but if the picture reproduces poorly it might keep people from inquiring about your offer. The best photos show yourself and family close up in the foreground with your home in the background. A nice auto in the picture can help, but leave out the pets. Readers want to think about vacationing while looking through the catalog, not feeding your dog. Focus must be sharp; 35mm camera with a wide angle lens will accomplish this. The picture should have high contrast — black blacks and white whites.

Possibly the single most effective action you can take to increase your chances of finding an ideal trading partner is to enclose an additional fee (usually two or three dollars) to pay for first-class postage delivery of your catalog. This cannot be over-emphasized. Timing is vital when thousands of hopeful exchangers all receive their catalogs within a couple of weeks of each other, worldwide. If you gain a week or two through the postal service you might have an advantage in contacting exchangers, making acquaintance, and agreeing to a deal.

The Initial Contact

In order to contact exchangers advertising in agency catalogs, it is not necessary that you list your home. For a reduced fee, agencies will send you their catalogs in which you haven't listed your home. Of course, this places all the responsibility for making contact on you. Other exchanges won't be aware of your desire to trade. But whether you list your home or not, contact with agency members is made in the same manner: by mail or telephone.

Contact by mail has several advantages over using the telephone. Letters are universally accepted as a proper, polite means of introduction, whereas calling someone you do not know can be interpreted as rude behavior. Writing a letter allows you to control your thoughts and expressions and plan so that you write exactly what you want to say. The postal services are less expensive than telephoning, and many times with international listings you will be unsure whether the exchangers in question speak your language.

Sometimes mailing your message is disadvantageous. Telephoning is increasingly accepted as a quick way to accomplish business. Since timing is so important in contacting partners, phoning can be justified if either a listing is too tempting to resist or if it's late spring and time is running out to agree to an exchange. Nothing is more heartbreaking than reading a marvelous listing and dashing off a letter, only to find out that they agreed to a swap just before your offer arrived.

You can speed up the relatively slow mailing process by pre-planning in anticipation of receiving your catalog. Why wait to find the listings that interest you and then plan your letter? By preparing ahead you'll have your letters in the mail a couple of days before the majority of exchangers. Here's what you'll need: 1. A good typewriter or computer printer with a new ribbon, 2. Typing paper, 3. Fifty #10 envelopes and 50 #9 envelopes, 4. Pre-printed return address labels, an address stamp, or printed stationery, 5. Stamps and possibly International Reply Coupons.

Your letter should be typed and either printed at a printer's shop, photocopied on a good copier, or dashed off on a computer printer. Have 50 copies made. You should make the letter appear as professional as possible by proofreading for spelling errors. Personalized stationery or good quality paper helps.

The writing style should be friendly and conversational. Write in first person dialogue and use personal pronouns such as you, we, I and your.

To make your letter stand out from the 20 or 30 other offers your potential partners are likely to receive, grab their attention. Keep their eyes glued to the page. This is best done by beginning your letter with a strong, intriguing "hook." Effective hooks are sentences, questions, startling statements or fragments designed to prick the reader's interest. Questions like, "I'm sure you've heard of Disneyland, but do you know where to find EPCOT Center, the colossal Disney park that's just as educational as it is fun?" or statements such as "Ireland is famous for rolling green hills and Waterford crystal, yet the mystery of Newgrange, a highly decorated underground tomb built 5,000 years ago by Stone Age man continues to stun visitors," work well to hook readers. Short sentences or fragments can be just as catchy: "Tokyo isn't really the world's second largest city; it's actually hundreds of tiny towns stacked together," and "Where's the capital of Montana?" will interest readers sufficiently to seriously consider your offer.

After your hook, you need to explain where you saw their listing, introduce yourself, briefly state your occupation and describe family members. Then you can elaborate on your surrounding area, weather, neighbors, popular local attractions, and your home. While asking if they'd be interested in exchanging with you in the letter's conclusion, it's a good idea to tie in the ending with your opening hook. Use simple words to avoid cross-cultural misunderstandings and avoid jargon and slang. Cliches may not be understood either. Following is a first contact letter incorporating these suggestions.

> Dear Mr. Mangrove:
> When was the last time you and your family feasted on freshly caught, fat pink salmon?
> After seeing your listing in the InterService Home Exchange directory, my husband and I couldn't help writing. Your home sounds terrific!
> I'm Jennie Fiche, and with my husband Norman I recently retired from teaching in Vancouver, British Columbia. We live in Victoria, the capital of British Columbia, Canada's loveliest province. The two of us are seeking a home exchange this summer, when Canadian weather is at its finest.
> Victoria is a truly royal city, exuding a distinctive British flair with the spaciousness and freshness of the Pacific Northwest. Surrounded by fashionable Victorian-style houses, Vancouver Island hosts enough tourist attractions — the Parliament Buildings, fireworks at the world renowned Butchart Gardens, Craigdarroch Castle — to keep even natives busy sight-seeing.
> Where our 1982 Volvo can't take you, the British Columbia ferries can, connecting the Island with the Sunshine Coast, where you can drive through the pine-covered coastal mountains and swim, sun, picnic, and camp. Seattle and the whole U.S. are only a quick ferry ride south.

One of the things Norman and I enjoy most is visiting the undeveloped hot springs at Knight Inlet, Flores Island, or Hot Springs Cove. Only locals know about these treasures! Soaking in warm water while sharing wine and cheese is the best way in the world to watch a Pacific sunset.

Our suburban three-bedroom, two-bath Victorian house is equipped with modern appliances and is centrally located in Victoria. I have a large, colorful flower garden, as many of the surrounding friendly neighbors do, and a spacious backyard.

Would you be interested in exchanging homes this summer? If so, please use the self-addressed, stamped envelope to send us information about yourself, your home, and surrounding area, or telephone if you'd prefer. Oh yes! About that fat, pink salmon: our next door neighbors have invited you to go ocean fishing with them on their boat, and they always catch plenty of delicious fish for a salmon barbecue Victoria-style.

Hope to hear from you soon,
Sincerely,

Jennie and Norman Fiche
address, telephone number

It is not uncommon for exchangers to tentatively arrange a swap for the following year if both parties like each other's offer but one family is already committed to another exchange this eyar. Mentioning this possibility in your letter may save you from marketing your home again next year.

Plan to mail about 50 copies of your letter as soon as you've received the exchange catalog. Individually type in each addressee's name after the salutation on each sheet, and have the 50 #9 envelopes pre-addressed to you. Stamp the return envelopes only if mailing within your country; otherwise, go to the post office and buy International Reply Coupons (coupon-response international) to include with the letter. Then when the catalog arrives you'll be ready to pick exciting offers and mail your letters right away.

That you have a full evening to look through the catalog as soon as it arrives is a must. Upon seeing the various offers your imagination is bound to race off to destinations you hadn't dreamed of going. Hazel Nayar's fine pamphlet, *Hints on Home-swapping,"* offers this advice from Great Britain:

"When our Exchange Book arrives, you will, of course, want to browse through it, but don't delay too long. Whatever you do, don't assume that someone is certain to write to you first: if everyone waits, nobody exchanges. Assume that *all* the initiative rests with you. As you browse, you should find a number of more or less suitable offers. Make a note of these and select perhaps half a dozen. One which seems perfect for you may not mention your region. Don't despair; it's often surprising where people will go with a little persuasion. One family who planned a holiday in France wrote to tell us they had been to Algeria instead, exchanging homes and cars, and venturing into the Sahara during their six weeks' stay."

If you plan on using the telephone to make initial contact with exchangers, you should prepare yourself much as if you were going to write them a letter. Jot down a list of area attractions, home attributes, and information about yourself. First impressions are terribly important. Be friendly and courteous while remembering to speak clearly and slowly if calling people in another country. If the call is long distance, don't ask them details about their home. Instead, ask them to mail you an information sheet on their home and surroundings, with the number of exchangers and preferred dates. Otherwise you'll have one huge phone bill!

After your initial conversation, immediately send a follow-up letter if their situation sounds inviting. Restate your situation in detail and tell them how much you enjoyed speaking with them.

Plan your calls so that you won't be calling during peak hours when rates are high. If dialing direct during low demand hours, a three-minute call from California to England can cost under three dollars. Leaf through the beginning of your phone book for dialing instructions, time zone charts (you really don't want to wake them up at 2:00 a.m., do you?), and the least expensive hours to call.

The More You Advertise, The More Inquiries You'll Get

To increase your opportunities you merely have to increase the advertising you do. You can supplement your agency ad by subscribing to more than one catalog, placing a newspaper ad with a paper that distributes in your first-choice destination, or sending notices to university departments. Each of these methods will cost a modest amount of money, maybe another $30-$50.

Two women I know beat the extra fee through an only slightly ingenious alternative: each subscribes to different agencies and when the catalogs arrive they simply share books and send out more letters.

Another way to get your offer to more people is to supplant the use of letters with postcards, such as this:

> Hello!
> We saw your home exchange advertisement in the Loan-A-Home catalog and find it very exciting. We also are in the catalog. If you find our listing attractive, please send a letter describing your home and surrounding area.
> We look forward to hearing from you soon,
>
> Mike Durke
> (address & telephone number)

Sending postcards doesn't allow you to "sell" your offer to prospective partners like a letter does, but it will enable you to reach up to 150 agency members for the same price as sending 50 letters. And even though your response ratio will be lower with postcards, it's worth considering if your catalog listing is attractive to readers.

You can type your brief message on a three-by-five inch card, and have 150 cards printed. Then you merely type or write their address on the front side. You might consider having a rubber return address stamp made, they're inexpensive and will save time. As with letters, have your postcards printed before the first agency catalog arrives. Some postal offices will sell pre-stamped cards which you can then take to the printer.

ADVICE ALERT
(from Ann Garry, Beverly Hills, California)

"INCLUDE ALL OF YOUR USUAL HOUSEHOLD SERVICE WORKERS IN THE EXCHANGE (E.G., CLEANING PEOPLE, GARDENER, POOL SERVICE). THEY NOT ONLY PROVIDE THE CUSTOMARY SERVICES, BUT THEY KEEP AN EYE ON THINGS."

Fifty letters, let alone 150 postcards, represents a great deal of correspondence. For organization and personal sanity it's helpful to write down a master list containing each catalog number that you've sent something to, and then start a separate file folder for each exchanger whom you begin writing with regularly. Photocopy each of the letters you write so that you'll have a record of what you've written and promised. These files can prove invaluable when, in years to come, you're desperately trying to remember which family it is that prefers winter vacations, or which couple is coming for a hospitality exchange next month (and when you're to pick them up at the airport).

Chapter 5

Alternative Advertising

Exchange agency listings are simply advertisements. Whenever you release information publicly about your desire to exchange, whether through an agency, newspaper, or university, or even at a cocktail party, you are advertising. This chapter deals with the less popular, alternative advertising channels. These alternative advertising forms reach a distinctive audience apart from home exchange agencies. But, the more advertising options you are aware of, the better your chances for finding an ideal exchange partner for each swap.

Do You Need A Different Audience?

Some people, due to their circumstances, may not be successful in finding a desirable partner through exchange agencies. If you answer "yes" to any of the following questions, choosing a different audience to advertise to may be advantageous for you:

1. Are you restricted to exchanging in only one area?
2. Does your home offer logistical advantages for businesspeople more so than for tourists?
3. Do you need a long-term (three or more months) exchange?
4. Will your offer appeal to people with narrow categorical interests such as skiing, golfing, archaeology, zoology, publishing, or politics?

5. Do you live near a well-known university?
6. Do you need an exchange quickly?
7. Will you agree to and enjoy a socially inequitable trade?
8. Is the area you want to exchange to considerably more popular with tourists than the area you'll be exchanging from?

A "Yes" doesn't mean that agencies will be useless. It means that other advertising channels may enable you to more accurately reach those people most likely to want an exchange with you. Here are some examples of how alternative advertising works.

Giuseppe, a New York City restaurateur, wanted to take his family to Italy to visit relatives. To avoid the hot summer, Giuseppe waited until July to start writing families listed in his friend's Vacation Exchange Club catalog, but because he had waited so long he didn't find a partner. Everyone he wrote had already taken their holidays or had agreed to upcoming exchanges, or were gone on vacation. Disappointed by trying to salvage his plans, Giuseppe wrote the newspaper *Stampa Sera* with a classified ad for an exchange partner and within 12 days had agreed to a swap. The newspaper ad cost Giuseppe one-half what the exchange book had cost his neighbor.

There are two important differences between advertising in an agency catalog and using an alternative source. A good exchange club organizer will go out of her way to assist you in finding a partner, if at first you are not successful. Secondly, more help and explanation from you might be required if you contact a partner through a newspaper, magazine, school, or community group, since that person may be completely unfamiliar with the concept and process of home exchanging. You will have to be extra careful to make all agreements, arrangements, and provisions clear.

Newspapers And Magazines

You might already be familiar with a magazine that has the type of audience you want to reach, or remember a newspaper that serves the area where you're going. That's great. But on the hunch that you'll still need addresses, telephone numbers, and sources of more publications, here are several widely available reference guides for magazines and newspapers that can be found at almost any library.

The annual *Ulrich's International Periodicals Directory* lists by subject both foreign and domestic magazines. Addresses and circulations are mentioned.

The Standard Periodical Directory lists by subject U.S. and Canadian magazines and newspapers, with addresses, telephone numbers, and circulations.

The IMS Ayer Directory of Publications lists by area publications in the U.S., Canada, Puerto Rico, Virgin Islands, Bahamas, Bermuda, and the Philippines, including addresses, telephone numbers, and circulations.

The annual *Writer's Market,* published by Writer's Digest Books, lists by subject U.S. and Canadian magazines, with a description of each periodical's readership, with addresses, telephone numbers, and usually circulation.

Newspaper circulations are especially important since placing a classified ad in a paper with 50,000 readers may cost the same as placing an ad with its cross-town rival, which boasts 75,000 readers. The larger papers usually provide the best value for your advertising money unless the smaller paper caters to a specific, desirable audience, such as upper class readers or retirees (these two classes of persons travel often). If you're not sure who reads which paper, analyze the advertisements from retailers. If the products are expensive luxury items, the readership is affluent. Appendix B lists largest newspapers geographically so that you may place classified ads with them directly.

It's wise to get a look at a magazine before sending in a check with your ad, both to make sure the readership is right for your offer and that they do indeed print classified ads. Many don't. Local bookstores stock magazines and major libraries have hundreds on hand for you to analyze.

Newspaper classified ads are probably more effective than magazine classifieds simply because people tend to associate classified ads with newspapers. So that's where they'll look first. Newspaper rates are generally less expensive, too.

Once you've found the right publication, you've got to write your ad. The ad needn't be elaborate or lengthy, as long as it satisfies these four criteria:

1. *Keep it short.* Magazines typically charge by the word, and newspapers by the line, so condense your ad as much as possible. A few adjectives will brighten the copy, but leave details out. These ads will not be nearly as inclusive as an agency catalog listing.
2. *Grab the reader's attention.* Same objective discussed in the last chapter (The Initial Contact). Hook 'em.

3. *Make it clear that you seek an exchange.* Most people will assume that there's a rental charge involved.
4. *Include your telephone number with your address.* On the whole, I've found that ads with telephone numbers listed are more successful than ads listing only an address or post office box. It seems that readers, excited at the spur of the moment by the opportunity to try something new will pick up the phone and call but if only an address is listed, they may contemplate the idea long enough to talk themselves out of writing at all.

Here's an example classified ad written for a large metropolitan newspaper:

FREE Home Exchange w/Florida
family June 1-30, near EPCOT,
P.O. Box 921, Orlando FL
32707 (305 333-1875)

More and more newspapers have classified categories for home rentals, travel, and exchanging. Here's one found in the *San Francisco Chronicle* under the category "Vacation Rentals":

Rent-Free Vacation!
Swap houses 2 wks in
Aug w Boston Area Family
Call 617 266-1010

For students, ads in campus newspapers often are read and are many times free:

International student at
Stanford seeks free room
& board with local family
in exchange for same with
family in Sao Paulo, Brazil this school year. Call
Bechtel
International Center, Stanford.

All three of these are examples of geography-specific general audience advertisements. Ads in specialty magazines, like *Arts Magazine,* read by artists, museum officials, and art teachers, or *International Musician,* read by union musicians, reach a specific audience.

The readers may be geographically dispersed, but all are interested in one particular topic. Following is an example home exchange ad in a musician's magazine slanted to especially interest musicians:

DIXIELAND FANS IN
EASTERN U.S.
cities: Swap houses with Sacramento
couple to enjoy world's biggest
DIXIE JAZZ JUBILEE, May 24-31.
A. Poot, 837 Miramar Rd., Sacramento CA 95821,
(916) 483-0128.

See how this ad zeros in on musicians with a narrow, specific interest? The lead wouldn't be nearly so effective if it read "Musicians in Eastern U.S. cities." You have to analyze exactly what is attractive in your area, and then find the precise audience; in this case, Dixieland jazz musicians and fans. The advertising couple pointedly asked for people living in eastern U.S. cities because that's where they wanted to go.

Advertisements in classified sections of business magazines or newspapers are similarly written, though with a business slant. Here's an ad written for the *Wall Street Journal:*

Want to investigate business
opportunities in NYC for free?
Exchange homes w NY family who wish to vacation
in S. Calif-L.A. area.
Dates open, 212 232-4937, Tom McReynolds.

If you're sending your ad to a magazine or newspaper printed in a foreign language, try to send the ad in the correct translation so that it will be ready to print. "I know a German woman who runs a deli where I shop," one exchanger told me. "I don't speak or write German so I showed her my ad in English and she wrote it in German right there for me," he said.

Think of friends or connections you know who might be willing to translate your ad. Language instructors at local high schools, colleges, and universities are more reliable, and, if approached cordially, will often help. Newspaper staffs will usually attempt to decipher your message if it is received untranslated, though you risk having the letter dropped in the trash can or forgotten about. Before sending your letter make sure the language you send the advertisement in is widely read by the populace. In many countries with their own language, English is as commonplace as the native tongue.

As a last resort there are commercial translation services who will gladly translate for a fee. Your telephone directory's Yellow Pages lists these firms under "Translations-Interpreters," and some addresses appear in the Appendix.

When your ad is in the proper language, send it to the publication with a cover letter of explanation, as follows:

June 1, 1986
Classified Ad Department
The Dallas Morning News
Communications Center
Dallas, TX 75265

Dear Ladies and Gentlemen:

Please run the enclosed advertisement in your classified section, under "Vacation Rentals" or a similar category you think appropriate. I am searching for a partner for a home-to-home exchange in the Dallas area.

Please bill me immediately for the advertisement.

Cordially,

Jim Dearing
(address and phone number)

Address envelopes "Classified Ad Department," "Attention: Classified Advertisements," or "Want and Sell Ads," in the appropriate language. Prices will depend on how long you wish the ad to run and how large the paper's circulation is. Metropolitan newspaper rates for one week vary from $4 to $70 and in magazinees from $25 to $50 for one issue. If placing an ad by telephone make sure you are fluent in the country's native language or have someone on your end of the line who is, so you won't waste the phone charge vainly trying to communicate with a receptionist.

Universities And Schools

The first place students, teachers, and others wanting to exchange homes or find a youth hospitality exchange through schools should turn to are campus international centers. The chances that the international center staff will have heard of anyone coming to the school wanting to exchange homes or rooms, and that they're coming from the area where you want to go, are slim. Still, if anyone will know, it's them. It's worth the minimal effort.

Assuming that your local school's international center staff can't find you a prospective partner, you'll need to know all the colleges and universities in the area you're going to, their addresses and telephone numbers, and contacts in their international centers. Your own international center will have this information as long as the school actively is involved in student exchanges.

For students the process is then fairly simple. First write the international centers at all the area schools, inquiring about any students coming to your area. Here's an example:

May 24, 1986
Michael J. Calo, Assistant Director
Division of International Programs
Syracuse University
Syracuse, NY

Dear Mr. Calo:

I am a student at the university in Strasbourg, and will be studying at Syracuse on a school sponsored program this school year.

I request a youth hospitality home-to-home exchange with a Syracuse student coming to Strasbourg. Can you help me?

He or she is welcome in my family if I am welcome in his or hers. This would save both of us accommodation money while enhancing our understanding of French and American home life.

Best wishes,

Bernard Boutte
26 rue Lorraine
45000 ILLKIRCH GRAFFENSTADEN
FRANCE

After writing international centers but before waiting for their responses, send classified advertisements to each main campus newspaper, to advertise directly to the student body. Below is an ad written for three Sacramento area college newspapers:

Studying in Eugene next year?
By trading bedrooms and living
with each other's families we could both save $$$!
Call Jill,
503 412-7081 to arrange.

ADVICE ALERT
(from Paul Loeser, Jr., Jackson, New Hampshire)
"STATE CLEARLY THE NUMBER AND KIND OF YOUR HOUSE PETS. EVEN IF THEIR CARE AND FEEDING HAS BEEN ASSUMED BY SOMEONE ELSE, THEY WILL DEMAND HOUSE ROOM AND ATTENTION WHICH CAN BE ANNOYING TO A NON-PET EXCHANGER. AN EXCESSIVE NUMBER OF HOUSE PLANTS TO BE WATERED CAN ALSO BE A DRAG IF NOT ANTICIPATED."

The first move for teachers or vacationers concerning school connections is the same as for students: the international centers at all schools within the area you're going to. Get the contact names from your own local international center and proceed to write, asking if they are aware of any faculty exchanging jobs to your area. At the same time, type up a notice to teachers that you will send to them via their department secretaries (your package should first be sent to the main administrative office with directions that it then be sent by inter-office mail to the department you specify). This next ad is from a professor at the University of Hawaii at Manoa:

Dear Instructor:
  This fall since I will be teaching at a university in your area, my family and I are looking for a partner going to Hawaii during this time to exchange homes.
  Our house is located three miles from the University of Hawaii

at Manoa on Honolulu. The house was built in the mid-sixties and is beautifully secluded by palm trees. Inside are three bedrooms and two baths, a modern kitchen, tv, stereo, bar.

We are willing to exchange our two cars, one a 1983 Honda Accord, the other an older Chrysler. Both run dependably.

I need to exchange between August 25 and December 20. We can stay longer if necessary for you.

If interested, please write me at the address above, or phone the number below.

Cordially,

Robert Chan, Ph.D.
(808) 2442-8244

Type your notice twice on one page, make photocopies, and then cut the pages in half. It will be nearly impossible to send enough notices for each school's entire faculty, so choose several departments at each school to send the notices to. Which departments should you pick? Send according to the strong points of your own school, so you'll reach professors more likely to be interested in teaching at your school (or at other schools in your home community). For example, if your campus is noted for its strong School of Business Administration and Economics Department, send notices to these departments of schools in the area you wish to visit.

The easiest and most reliable way to have these notices properly distributed is to first call each school's international center and ask the names of the appropriate department secretaries and the faculty size of the respective departments. Then divide the notices into the correct numbers for each department, bind them together with a personally typed explanatory cover letter addressed to the secretary asking her to distribute these notices in faculty mail boxes, and then label each small bundle with the secretary's name and department, such as "Betty Wolfman, Journalism Department."

Put these several bundles in a large manila envelope and mail it to the general administration office of the school. Repeat this process for each school in the area.

Community Host and International Visitor Services

The purpose of community host organizations and local international visitor service groups is usually to enable governments or institution sponsored guests from abroad to meet community citizens. Most visits only last two to three days, so host organizations are not in the practice of finding long-term accommodations for visitors let alone home exchange partners. Nevertheless, if approached properly, many of these groups will try to help teachers and students coming to their area find a home or hospitality exchange partner.

ADVICE ALERT
(from Ernest Mitchell, Philadelphia, Pennsylvania)

"SIZE UP THE PEOPLE BY THE TONE AND COMPOSITION OF THEIR LETTERS. AFTER YOU HAVE AGREED TO EXCHANGE WITH SOMEONE, FIND OUT WHAT THEY WANT TO DO AND SEE IN YOUR AREA. THEN GATHER ALL THE MAPS AND INFORMATION THAT YOU CAN FOR THEM. MAKE SURE YOU LEAVE A HAND DRAWN MAP OF YOUR NEIGHBORHOOD SHOWING WHERE STORES, HOSPITALS, AND HIGHWAYS ARE LOCATED."

Members of international visitor groups are usually upper income people who are experienced travelers themselves. They involve themselves in friendship groups because through travel they've been exposed to various cultures and they appreciate the need for better cross-cultural communication. Thus, the memberships of these groups are an excellent audience for you to reach. Many of them have exchanged homes before.

Because the volunteer groups themselves are a potential source of exchangers, teachers shouldn't just advertise for teachers, and students shouldn't only look for other students already coming to their area. If you're an instructor, ask these groups whether any members would like to exchange homes for vacationing or business reasons. Students should describe the attributes of their school and culture, and ask members in their letter whether they'd like to send their own son or daughter to take part in a youth hospitality exchange.

Your request for a home or hospitality exchange partner will not be a standard arrangement — possibly not even a known concept — for them, so you will have to explain the process. This can easily be done in an explanatory letter of introduction like this:

February 9, 1986

Director
World Affairs Council of Rhode Island
Providence, RI
To Whom It May Concern:

I am wondering if you can help me.

I have been invited to teach the 1986-87 school year at Williams High School in Providence, on a paid leave of absence from my own school here in Oxford, England. I look forward to visiting your community.
In order to save money and further appreciate the lifestyle you enjoy in the States, I have been trying, unsuccessfully I might add, to find a homeowner in Providence who would like to exchange houses with me for this period. My wife will be coming with me, along with our ten-year-old boy who will attend school in Providence. We will be glad to exchange houses and autos with a family in your town. An exchange of homes is a time honored tradition involving no exchange of money. Both parties must be willing to assist the other, and be respectful of the home they are living in.

If you could please circulate the enclosed notice among your members I would be deeply appreciative (maybe it could be reproduced in a flyer?) I can be contacted at the address below.

Thank you for help.

Sincerely,

Robert Kent
(address)

A notice to the group's membership should be enclosed so that your cover letter won't have to be rewritten by the group director. It's a good idea to ask members in the notice to tell their friends of your offer if they themselves are not interested. Leave yourself as much time as possible to find a partner. Find out the addresses of community organizations as soon as you know you'll be going, and get those letters in the mail.

Chapter 6

Making An Offer They Can't Refuse

After you've taken the first step of advertising your home, you need to prepare for the second step which is correspondence. Inquiries by telephone and mail are going to begin trickling (flooding?) in. To consummate a deal quickly before all the best offers are taken, it's smart to be prepared to mail out a complete packet on your home and self as soon as people respond to your ads.

After interested people send you similar information you'll have time to ask questions and form a better idea of offers and the people involved. People might write or call before you've received your home exchange agency catalog, so you've got to be able to spin on your heels and drop a pre-packaged Total Offer in the mailbox. Immediately. That means all the package components have to be completed and ready to go. What are the components that make up an irresistible offer? You'll need attractive photographs of your surrounding area attractions, your home, and your family; tourist pamphlets describing the local sights; a road map, showing home proximity to attractions, schools, and downtown districts; professional references and, if available, references from previous exchange partners; and two optional photocopied documents, a home real estate appraisal and a personal credit check.

Home Packets

Mailing photos, as many as feasible of yourself, your home, and the surrounding area, is one of the easiest transfers of proof exchange partners can make. You should send pictures of yourself and anyone accompanying you on the exchange whether family, friends, or business acquaintances. If you're a student exchanging hospitality, include photos of your family, so that the other youth exchanger can get an idea of who he'll be living with.

Take care to send plenty of pictures of your home. Take several from the outside, each at a different angle, so that your partners can see the structure of the home. For an apartment or small office, one outside shot will suffice. A photo of each room should be included, and each automobile should be pictured. Any unusual or extravagant items should be pictured, such as snowmobiles, swimming pools, boats, satellite receiving dishes, or personal computers. Photographs of the surrounding area add a touch of identity to your home. A few photos of nearby popular tourist attractions, lakes, mountains, or big cities all help to impress the idea that you live in an area worthy of visiting.

You needn't be a professional photographer or have expensive photographic equipment, but the sharper and more attractive your photos, the better. Pay attention to composition, and focus your lens or brace the camera carefully to avoid blurry results. One 20-exposure roll of color film will provide enough exposures to highlight what you have to offer. If you have access to a 35 mm camera, use it or find someone who can.

Cast yourself in the right light, too. If your partners receive pictures of your lounging around, hair out of place and wearing an old, filthy T-shirt, what impression will they get? Perhaps that you're not very well-kept, and might not take loving care of their home. Appear well-groomed and neatly dressed, and smile. Your partners want to like you. Make it easy for them.

Similarly, the pictures you take of your home and area should be complimentary. Highlight those things which make your home and location attractive and distinctive. A friend of mine owns a small cabin in Montana which is nice but by no stretch of the imagination ornate.

Instead of concentrating his photographs on the cabin, he took a stunning picture of the Big Hole River, a blue ribbon trout stream that meanders through his property. By advertising that photograph in a fishing and hunting magazine he was swamped with offers from interested exchangers. By playing up the strong points without misrepresenting your offer you'll attract more attention.

Since photographs require lab time for developing and printing, don't wait until you receive exchange offers to take your pictures. You'll lose a week or two. Begin taking pictures when you place your classified ads, or just before the agency list you subscribe to is due for publication. It's wise to order ten to twenty copies of each good photo, since it's quite likely you'll send out more than one set of pictures (and you can always use extras in coming years).

To supplement the photographs you send highlighting area attractions, include a city or county map to show your home's proximity to those attractions. Also, a map will clearly show road access and road conditions to your home. Be sure to mark where your home is and where area attractions are on the map. If you're a member of the American Automobile Association or equivalent road service you may be entitled to an unlimited supply of free maps.

If you're uneasy about "hyping" your area's worthiness, or feel that it really doesn't have much to offer, visit your local chamber of commerce. They'll have free brochures describing your locale in sparkling hyperbole. And by sifting through pamphlets you'll probably run across historical or unusual local tourist attractions that you weren't aware existed. These brochures are free, so get enough (again, ten to twenty for starters) to send to each interested exchanger.

All three of these types of proof — photographs, maps, and travel brochures — you should likewise request from prospective partners. They're your tangible evidence that the home is acceptable and that the area is functional or interesting.

The most influential type of reference letter you can have is one written by a former exchange partner. This alone can carry enough weight to relieve any apprehension the other party may have about leaving their home with you. For example:

Dear Fellow Home Exchanger,

I write this letter on the behalf of Dana and Dave Halen. In August of 1984 my husband and I exchanged houses with the Halens and had a delightful time. Not only were Dave and Dana helpful to us before the exchange, but during the vacation they called us twice, asking if everything was all right and letting us know how our vegetable garden was producing and that our dog was fine.

I am positive that any exchange you have with them will turn out fine. When Tim and I returned home after six weeks our house was in excellent condition, just as we had left it. The lawns were even newly mowed.

Sincerely,

Nancy Lindsay
916 726-4849
Roseville, California

If you are not able to get a letter of reference from past exchange partners but they would still recommend you, list their names, addresses, and telephone numbers on a reference page that you can then photocopy. Of course you'll need the permission of the past exchangers to make sure they don't mind being listed as a reference. Another type of reference useful to beginning exchangers is a personal or professional letter of reference. Here's an example

---

January 13, 1986

To Whom It May Concern:
I have been a legal council for Mr. and Mrs. Barney Rife for 13 years. During this time I have found them both to be of high morals and good character. They have always been honest and forthright to the best of my knowledge.

You may call me at the number below if so desired.

I remain,

John Radakovitz, Attorney-at-Law
Member: Minnesota State Bar

Even though personal and professional references are perfectly valid they will not be as reassuring as a letter from a former exchange partner, someone who has been in the position that your potential partners are contemplating.

A photocopied real estate appraisal of your home and property is a nice touch to your package of photos, tourist pamphlets, maps, and references. It's a thoughtful assurance for your partner. Unfortunately, appraisals also are expensive. If your home has been appraised within the past ten years, send a copy of the appraisal with a note that it's out of date, if indeed it is. Otherwise a new appraisal will cost anywhere from $50 to $150. Should you pay for one? First consider who your likely partner will be. Teachers, students, and people on business rarely care whether the home they're visiting is worth as much as the home they're vacating, since they're swapping primarily for location and access. To them the home might only function as a place to eat and sleep. Vacationers, on the other hand, might feel cheated if they had intended on spending a great deal of time in the home and it turns out to be of lesser value than their own.

Getting a credit check on yourself is also a reassurance for potential partners, since some bills may have to be settled after you've returned home. Look in the Yellow Pages under "Credit Reporting Agencies" and request a validation of your own credit rating. Cost is approximately ten dollars.

These components, along with a personal letter from you, comprise the offer to possible partners that follows your initial contact letter. If you haven't received a similar package from interested people, request one in your personal cover letter, like this:

March 3, 1985

Dear Frank & Lynn:

We were delighted to receive your letter of interest for arranging a home exchange. We think a vacation in Alberta would be fabulous!

We are sending you photographs of our home, area, and our family, along with maps, brochures, and copies of our property appraisal and personal credit report. Also we've added a reference from the school principal where we both teach.

Can you please send us similar materials so that we may more fully judge your offer?

We are sure you would find your stay in San Diego enjoyable!

We have received other exchange offers, and we want to make a decision within two or three weeks so that everyone has time to make an exchange. Please write soon since you are our first choice.

We look forward to hearing from you soon,

Dean and Simone Popien

Appraisals And Credit Ratings

If you do not feel confident that a potential partner is telling the truth, you probably should not exchange with him. If, however, he represents a swap opportunity that you absolutely need (such as a teacher who has only one offer from the area where he'll teach with time running short), you can request a real estate appraisal as long as you also are willing to send an appraisal of your home.

You should be wary of direct real estate comparisons if the properties are not located in the same type of area. Big city values are high, with high-traffic vacation spots even higher. For instance, a sprawling, five-bedroom home on two acres of land in Calgary, Alberta valued at $120,000 may be four times larger and indeed much nicer than an apartment in Honolulu; yet, due to market demand the apartment may be valued at $300,000. If you're going to compare property value, the area the homes are in also must be taken into consideration.

If you have friends or relatives in the area perhaps they can drive by the home. Ask them to report back to you with their opinion. Knowing someone who will do this for you is really invaluable since they can tell you in an impartial way how nice the neighborhood is, whether the automobile looked new, how close the home is to the campus, or how long it will take to commute to the town business district.

Some bills may have to be settled after you've returned to your own home, such as the last month's telephone and utility charges. How can you make sure they'll pay for the bills they accumulated at your home? You can't. However, you can be assured which United States citizens normally do pay their bills by applying for a credit check at a credit reporting agency. Most credit agencies are members of either Credit Bureaus, Inc. or the PRW credit reporting agency, both of which link local agencies together by computer so that you may request credit information about someone in another state. It is up to each individual agent's interpretation of the 1970 Fair Credit Reporting Act to decide whether home exchangers qualify to receive credit reports on other people.

Questions To Ask Exchangers

Even after receiving photographs, references, and pamphlets from prospective exchangers you'll still have questions before deciding on a partner. If exchangers are listed in an agency catalog you have, you'll have some additional information on their offer. If not, formulate questions about the items listed in chapter four under the Trans-Lingual Abbreviation Code.

Two pertinent points are the number of guests and the exchanger's intended use of your home.

How many people will be coming to stay in your home? It's unnerving, a week before the swap, to hear your partner mention "Oh, I almost forgot! Is it okay if my brother and his family stay at your place too?" You shouldn't be confronted with last minute additions which might contribute to over use of your home. Are they being honest with you? Did they have this in mind all along? Four unexpected people sharing your home is certainly grounds for negotiating a quick rental fee in addition to the swap, though compensation can lead to trouble.

Why does each potential swapper want to stay in your home? Will it be used as a base from which to travel, or simply as a home? Maybe a business office to entertain clients? A small plantation to grow and harvest marijuana? Eliciting information about how your home will be used will help you to pick the right partner. Following are additional questions you may want the answers to:

1. How much land is your home situated on?

2. What is the immediate surrounding area like?

3. Do you own the home?

4. If you don't own the home, has the idea been cleared with the owner?

5. What is the square footage?

6. When was it built?

7. Do you have a car for exchange?

8. What brand, model, and year is it?

9. How expensive is fuel for the car?

10. Would it be all right if we toured in the car?

11. What is your age, occupation, and employment history?

12. How many people will be coming with you, and can you please describe them?

13. What is your educational background?

14. What interests you about this area?

15. When do you want to trade, and is this time period changeable?

16. How long have you lived in your current home?

17. Do you have family in your area?

18. Do you have friends, relatives, or neighbors that will be able to help us if we need it?

19. Do you have any commitments where you are that might interfere with exchanging homes?

20. Is there any reason you might have to prematurely end the exchange and expect to come home?

21. Can you purchase airline tickets ahead of time, as we will, and send a copy of your ticket receipts as insurance that you'll go through with the swap?

You should remain optimistic that everything will turn out fine but at the same time retain a pragmatic objectivity about what you are told. Concerning the surrounding area and home, for example, ask yourself, "Is the place everything it's cracked up to be?" Maybe the apartment *is* only a ten-mile drive from the university, but is the road quick and sure or unpaved and ridden with switchbacks? What does she really mean by "secluded and gorgeous?" Does the study really have a "professional, IBM-compatible personal computer," or is the computer actually an Atari that only plays games? The only way to be sure is to ask questions. Open, frank communication will prevent problems and misunderstandings, making you fully aware of the situation you'll be entering.

Working With An Interpreter

Advertising in a foreign country will often result in language barriers: you speak French but no German; your partner wrote you back in German and doesn't speak French. Or you speak and write English but your potential swapper speaks and writes Italian and understands only a bit of English, but plenty of French. Problems.

English is the world's international language, there can be no doubt of that. Obviously, however, anything you understand of other languages will help to defuse confusion. A language barrier will complicate matters and lengthen the time needed to reach consensus. Language problems quite possibly can make preparations exciting and fun and also can result in closer friendships. People who don't understand each other well tend to try very hard and tend to be especially polite. A degree of linguistic ambiguity adds flavor to your vacation!

ADVICE ALERT
(from C.R. Olsen, Leawood, Kansas)

"CONFIRM ARRANGEMENTS IN WRITING AFTER COMMUNICATING OVER THE PHONE. DEFINE RESPONSIBILITIES THAT ARE REQUESTED, SUCH AS PAYING ANY HIRED HELP, CARING FOR PETS, AND THE AUTOS."

The amount of misunderstanding can easily snowball though, so bringing in a third party to interpret is suggested if you're unsure that everything is being understood. If you're going to pay for a free-lance interpreter, ask to see verification of their credentials or proof of fluency. There's nothing worse than paying an interpreter to further knot the already twisted lines of communication. Payment, if any, should be shared equally by both parties, not shouldered by the partner who hires the interpreter. Make sure your partner agrees to this ahead of time, however.

If you choose to locate a go-between, prepare a list of vital questions, and have the interpreter discuss these points over the telephone with the partner. This will be expensive, but it's important to mutually agree on things quickly and with full two-way understanding.

It should be understood and agreed upon from the outset that each exchanger will be responsible for providing all lists, advice, and household instructions in the other exchanger's language. In such trades it is almost a necessity that each partner also find a neighbor to designate as a "primary reference," someone to be available intermittently to help the newcomers around the home and area.

Interpreters and, later, arranging for someone fluent in your guest's language to help them are but options. The vast majority of yearly exchanges involve no such "expert" intermediaries, the partners preferring to accept — even welcome — the cultural and lingual uncertainties. Surprises and overcoming problems can contribute to a satisfying and exciting vacation.

Do It Quick

Considering offers, getting to know potential partners, and agreeing to an exchange sounds like a lengthy process. In fact, everything has to happen very fast, especially if you are contacting and being contacted through home exchange agency catalogs. Three or four weeks is it. After that, the better, more popular offers will be taken. Don't mistake this for a passive sport. You've got to act aggressively while remaining polite and courteous. Have your photos taken, lists typed, stamps on the envelopes. Exchangers living in less popular areas — despite how beautiful the countryside or stunning the house — have to try even harder by sending more letters, making more phone calls, and doing it all a little sooner.

Never disregard using the telephone to make an initial contact if you're pressed for time. Send letters First Class or Airmail (Luftpost, Par Avion). Don't go any slower. Express Mail or Federal Express services are very expensive but your materials will get there the next day, if the offer is important enough to you. Special Delivery within the U.S. is still quick, moderately priced, and most importantly lets the other person know that his is an offer you're serious about.

Pressing or nagging exchangers to send letters sooner or send more information may give the wrong impression about you. Too many demands will encourage others to pass you by. If they're serious, they'll make the appropriate effort to keep in touch. Remember: different people, even those within the same society, move at different speeds. Lastly, don't take all my promptings to act with swiftness as a do-or-stay-at-home choice. Many exchangers delay their actions or experience time-consuming problems and still manage to find perfectly satisfying partners. Speed simply gives you an advantage.

Chapter 7

The Five Thousand Mile Handshake

Many exchangers excitedly accept the first offer they receive with little or no hesitation whatsoever — that's the ideal circumstance. This chapter is primarily for those situations when you have several offers from anxious exchangers and you can't decide which one to accept.

The one important rule in home exchanging is that once you have decided which offer to accept, it is imperative that you do so with resolve. Going back on one's word for whatever reason (especially receiving a late, preferable offer) is akin to sacrilege among home exchangers. Such a capricious action on the part of an exchanger typically has a calamitous effect on the victimized partner. Plans have been made, tickets bought, schedules aligned. Commitment is an inveterate law of exchanging. In fact, it is usually understood as incumbent upon the partner backing out of an agreement to find a substitute neighbor willing to exchange or, failing that, offer the distressed family free hospitality in their home. Courteous treatment is expected of all partners (and if you do receive a late, especially enticing offer, arrange a swap with that exchanger for next year).

Risk-Taking

Any home exchange involves a degree of risk. Minimizing this risk is best accomplished by open and frequent communications with potential partners so that you can feel comfortable with the partner you choose and consequently enjoy your vacation. There are several types of risk at work here. The most obvious and worried about, yet least likely to result in disaster, is the risk to your home and property. The amount of concern is expected since we all protect our possessions. Yet the vast majority of experienced exchangers would tell you not to waste too much time worrying about the belongings you place in the care of your partners. The aura of friendship fostered in exchange relationships typically behooves participants to treat each other's home gingerly.

Another more likely risk is the possibility of being disappointed or disillusioned with your partner's home once you get there. Housekeeping standards may not be what you're accustomed to. The Subaru may not afford the same luxury that your Lincoln does. These, of course, are matters that you can anticipate through questioning your partner on the phone. Conversation, particularly with international exchangers, should be interpreted literally. If the woman says her home includes a washer, postal service, and a swimming pool, don't immediately assume that she means an automatic washer, door to door postal delivery, and a private pool. That's not what she said. It might be a manual washer (with clothesline dryer), a mile hike to the postal box, and a communal pool.

Then again everything could be first-class and much nicer than what you're used to, which raises a third risk: guilt. This is not uncommon. Some conscientious exchangers slightly over-sell their homes in the name of advertising and then feel absolutely terrible upon arriving at their partner's more expensive home that is everything it was cracked up to be. As you can imagine this makes the guilt-ridden partner feel just wonderful for the remainder of the vacation. The risk of ruining your trip because of guilt is easily guarded against by simply telling the truth. Make sure your partner understands what your home is like.

Some people are uncomfortable asking for information and avoid asking questions which could be interpreted as personal, such as "What do you usually eat?", "Can you leave these things for us?", and "Is it all right to sleep in your bed, and do you have blankets, towels, and linens?" It's fine not to ask details such as these, but your exchange will proceed smoother and with fewer interruptions if you take the time to agree on details with your partner.

Comparing Potential Partners

Compared to judging personalities, weighing home offers is easy. But consider personalities we must, since almost all satisfying swaps are the product of satisfying friendships. Besides asking possible partners questions, there are questions you should ask yourself. Which person is the easiest to get along with? The friendliest? Ask yourself questions pertaining to the following categories:

Reliability. Try to ascertain, through as many letters and phone calls as possible, the reliability and promptness of each prospect. Were letters sent with all the information you requested? Did they do what they said they would do? Were phone calls returned promptly, and preliminary promises kept? At this early stage in your relationship you won't have much to go on, so pay attention to small personality clues that you might normally overlook or dismiss. Some people, you'll find, are really honest but have the disturbing habit of committing peccadillos that they brush off as irrelevant. It's not that they'll sell your furniture, it's just that they didn't pay to have their car tuned up like they promised, opting instead to let a kid down the street take a crack at it. Although there is a positive correlation between age and responsibility, it shouldn't be assumed that every 55-year-old is a safer bet than a 28-year-old.

Honesty. You'll be trying to decide whether the people are honest and can be completely trusted. I know one vacationing retired couple who exchanged their California home with two young girls for the summer. When the retired couple returned, they found that some of their furniture had been abused. The retirees hadn't spent adequate time corresponding with the girls, and thus didn't know whether they were honest and responsible. They had trusted them only on the basis of faith, which, in this unusual case, wasn't enough. Pay attention to why people want to exchange, how many of them want to come, and their description of their own home. Sometimes dishonest people will reveal themselves through inconsistencies over the period of correspondence.

Congeniality. Because arranging a swap does involve a substantial time commitment, it helps if you like the person you're dealing with. Exchanging should be an integrative process in which each of you assists the other. Exchanging with someone who's naturally friendly, open to conversation, and explains things in detail may not guarantee their integrity, but it's a positive indicator of a satisfying relationship. Comments from many experienced exchangers reveal that they keep swapping homes more for the friendships than for the vacationing experience. Whereas the vacations you'll enjoy are transient in nature, the friendships tend to remain intact. Accordingly, you should choose exchange partners primarily on friendliness. Choose the family you would most want to spend a vacation with, as if you were going somewhere together. If you're a student exchanging rooms, you'll need to pick a partner who will get along well with your family (since they'll be saddled with the person you choose).

Considerateness. Find a partner who is considerate of your needs—it's a quality required for a successful swap. Try to judge who will prepare the most thoroughly for you prior to the swap and who will most likely respect your belongings as if they were their own. At its best, home exchanging involves partners who work beforehand to increase each other's understanding, comfort, and pleasure during the swap. It's a team effort, and you should act as a responsible member of that team for your mutual benefit. That benefit and commitment isn't inherently short-lived, either. My wife stayed as a hospitality guest with a Japanese family for ten months. Subsequently, the Japanese came to stay with us in California for two weeks and we have returned and stayed with them for ten days. Now we have an informal understanding that when the Japanese couple's daughter is old enough, she will come to California and stay with us while attending an American school. Our lives are now inextricably woven together in a distant though strong friendship.

After weighing these categories, it is still important to remember that language misunderstandings, and to a greater degree, societal differences, sometimes make ambiguous situations. Letters might be slow in arriving, conditions mulled over, and agreements not immediately reached, simply because different societies move at different speeds (even within the same country). A New Jersey stockbroker might interpret a Saudi Arabian professor's leisurely attitude to indicate a lack of commitment when in fact it might only reflect the Saudi's way of life. An American's preoccupation with home security and apprehensiveness about others may well strike a Japanese exchanger as suspicious. Try to be open-minded.

But, be wary of holding out for an exchange with a partner whose offer is marvelous but whose commitment is definitely wishy-washy. Chances are good that that person also is holding out because of an offer he considers preferable to yours. Go instead with someone who sounds genuinely excited about coming to stay in your home. The latter's commitment won't waver and cause any ticket cancellations.

ADVICE ALERT
(J.A.B., New Orleans, Louisiana)
"ASK FOR A LIST OF NAMES AND ADDRESSES OF PREVIOUS EXCHANGE PARTNERS AND CONTACT AT LEAST ONE FAMILY ON THE LIST FOR REFERENCE PURPOSES."

Rating Your Options

Why you're swapping determines the importance you'll assign various criteria for rating offers. Not everyone sees a trade the same way. The following Exchange Comparison Chart attempts to illustrate this point, making the offers you receive a bit more graphic and thus, easier to choose from.

This chart uses six exchange criteria: proximity of each home in relation to school or work; currency exchange rate; exchanger personalities, including how much you like and trust them; home features and attractions; weather, temperature and the season when the prospects wish to swap; and tourist or area attractions.

To use the Exchange Comparison Chart to rate your options, first number the six criteria according to how important you deem each one. For instance, a retired couple based in Florida may want to drive their RV to one of several places where they've contacted home exchangers. How would they rate the six criteria (home to work proximity, currency exchange, personality, home attraction, climate and season, and area attractions)? Let's suppose they are experienced vacationers who want to go to a place where there's a lot to see and do, in a cooler climate. They appreciate staying in a nice, well-kept home and making new friends. Currency exchange doesn't matter since they're not leaving the country, and the same can be said of home proximity to work: it doesn't apply to them since they're vacationing. They might rate the six criteria like this:

1. Area Attractions
2. Climate and Season
3. Personalities
4. Home Attraction
5. Currency Exchange
6. Home to Work Proximity

A vacationer going out of the country on a limited budget would list currency exchange higher. Someone who is planning to spend a great deal of time in the home would rate home attraction higher. A teacher trading jobs would likely rate these criteria in exact opposite fashion.

To rate your offers, first discern the importance of these criteria to you on the one to six scale, in descending order of importance. Next, assign each a point value from 60 to ten points, as shown below (with your own ranking inserted):

1. Area Attractions   60 points
2. Climate and Season   50 points
3. Currency Exchange   40 points
4. Personalities   30 points
5. Home Attraction   20 points
6. Home to Work Proximity   10 points

To demonstrate how to apply this to offers you'll receive, let's look at how our retired Florida couple with the RV would rate offers they received from three other retired couples.

Burton	McIntosh	Johnson	
60	40	50	1. Area Attraction (60)
30	40	50	2. Climate And Season (50)
20	30	40	3. Personalities (40)
30	10	20	4. Home Attraction (30)
0	0	0	5. Currency Exchange (0)
0	0	0	6. Home To Work Proximity (0)
140	120	160	

This comparison allows our retirees one method for choosing which swap is the best for them. By the results they would exchange with the Johnsons. If you have more than three offers, raise the points awarded to twice the number of criteria used, multiplied by ten. Thus if the above example had four offers to compare the point importance would 120, 110, 100, 90, 80 and 70.

A method of rating offers like this isn't meant to supplant your intuitive judgment about partners. It is simply a tool to enable you to more clearly see what each partner is offering you in comparison to the others. Use it if you can't decide.

Compensating The Deal

Sometimes potential partners become interested in each other's offer, but one partner owns a considerably more valuable home. How to equalize the situation may be your question.

Cash compensation could be a supplement to the exchange and superficially this appears to be an equitable solution. In practice, however, the charging of compensation does much to transform the contributory, warm-hearted feeling between exchangers into something utilitarian, indeed avaricious.

The partner paying compensation can quickly come to think and act as a renter. While paying $150 a week in addition to exchanging their home it's not difficult for many people to reason that "We're paying for it, so let's *use* it!" That attitude is easily capable of abuse. Those paying feel less responsible for your belongings. Trust no longer governs the relationship. It becomes a monetary association.

Naturally, this change affects more than the exchange itself; it carries over into the post-exchange period as well. Enduring friendships are much less likely in this buyer-seller atmosphere.

The obvious solution is that those with higher-valued homes simply should not ask for any cash compensation. That's good insurance that their property will be taken care of. But other inventive solutions are possible too: the partner with the lower-valued home can offer free hospitality for the other family at a later date as well as the exchange, or special arrangements can be made by the lower-valued home owner, such as arranging for laundry service, baby-sitters, yard workers, or an extra vehicle, all prepaid. Perhaps a cabin or beach home can be offered in addition to the normal home. Of course, politeness on the part of the higher-valued home owner suggests that home value discrepancies not be brought up at all. Traveling down the socio-economic ladder may be as educational as traveling up.

Teachers, Students, and Other Long Term Stays

Since exchange motives of educators, students, and other long-term stays are quite different from those of vacationers, there are different prerequisites for picking partners. Time in which to arrange the exchange is a bigger concern since these exchangers must make other arrangements in addition to finding a home exchange partner. Teachers must contact and apply to teach at the school of their choice and be accepted as guest faculty, or be offered a position. They may have to apply for instructional grants to fund extracurricular research. Students wanting to exchange bedrooms or apartments are involved in the time-consuming task of filling out an endless stream of forms for school application, eligibility of course credit, teacher permissions, and financial aid and student loans — in addition to preparing to study abroad. This means that the exchange of homes must go as smoothly as possible so that the many other matters can be concentrated on.

These added duties cannot preclude responsibilities to the exchange partner. Even if you are not in it for the culture, you must accommodate your partner. That's the spirit that makes home exchanging work.

Students, though primarily exchanging for access to a school, are usually just as excited about the cultural opportunities as their education requirements; thus they usually make sure the transition for their partner is comfortable since they expect reciprocal assistance in cultural preparation.

There are educational networks through which teachers can exchange jobs and homes, some of which are listed in the Appendix. But while it is convenient to have an educational network find you a home exchange partner, choice of home exchange partners is almost always limited to your job exchange partner. Partners are chosen with little or no consideration given to personal compatibility. This isn't the fault of the organizations; they haven't the resources or a large enough exchange program to offer you a list of teachers or other people who want an exchange in your area. Rather, it's just a condition of going through educational exchange programs. These services can be a wonderful method of getting a foreign teaching job, but inflexibility regarding homes results in many instructors renting a place. You may want to advertise your home's availability yourself. Other long-term stays may be for various business reasons. These can take special note of the following although directed towards teachers and students.

The number one teacher objective is typically finding a home that is close to the campus or research center where you'll be working. Since you'll probably spend almost all of your time on campus, proximity of home to campus is important if only for the reasons of saving time and providing convenience.

Access, whether in form of an automobile, train, bus, bicycle, or by foot, must be available and reliable. A car might not be of any importance whatsoever if your temporary home is only a quarter of a mile from campus, but if a 40-minute one-way commute is the norm, transportation becomes a very big factor when deciding with whom to exchange homes. Ask the time it takes to commute, not just the distance. One university professor I know exchanged to a home 14 miles from the school where he was to teach, but had made sure that his exchanger had a reliable car for him to drive. However, the 14-mile stretch, though a spectacular, bucolic drive along California's coastal highway, proved to be slow and arduous due to record rainfall the previous winter that had caused the road to collapse in several places. Construction crews, one-lane detours, and bumper-to-bumper traffic transformed the 14 miles into a 45-minute headache. If the professor had inquired a bit more about road conditions and access, he most likely would have chosen another exchange partner and avoided the problem.

Privacy is important to many teachers, especially if you won't have an office provided at the school. If you are promised an office at school, inquire if it's a noisy cubicle shared with three other instructors. If so, a private study at home might be a priority.

Lugging around your own IBM is no fun, so ask about a typewriter in the home. If the exchanger doesn't have one to meet your needs, ask him to find out where you can rent one for a reasonable price. (It's also well worth asking your new department secretary about a spare typewriter, and whether there is a machine in your department office.) If you've got your own word processor you'll probably want to bring it. Nevertheless it might be convenient to ask your exchanger if he has a word processor that uses compatible software with yours — then neither of you would have to move the screens, power units, and printers.

The standard questions for vacationers listed in chapter six apply to teachers as well, but educators need some additional information about their new situation to ease the transition. It is essential that you have answers to questions before leaving.

Following is a list of subjects in addition to details of your particular teaching assignment, that you should gather information on from your temporary department secretary, department chair, or your school contact there. If you will be exchanging jobs with another teacher, he should be responsible for getting this information to you just as you are responsible for sending him the same information about your situation. The list is from the U.S. Department of Education's publication, *A Handbook for U.S. Exchange Teachers*, Fulbright Teacher Exchange Branch.

School
1. Total enrollment in school/college
2. Number of faculty members in school/college
3. Average size of elementary/secondary/college classes
4. Socio-economic level of students
5. Hours of school day
6. Length of class periods
7. Facilities for lunch and approximate cost
8. Location in relation to shopping, business, residential areas

Transportation (Private and Public) and Community Services
1. Size and type of community (urban, suburban, rural)
2. Modes of transportation to and from school (car pool, public transportation)
3. Public transportation and distances to and from shopping areas
4. Names and locations of best places to buy basic needs and items unique to your city/region
5. Names and locations of other places of importance (libraries, churches, recreation facilities)
6. Climate and type of clothing needed
7. Cultural activities and sites of interest

Children's Schooling
1. Location of schools (private and public) in relation to housing and teaching assignment
2. Transportation facilities and approximate cost to and from schools
3. Documents, including transcripts and medical examination forms required for enrollment
4. Tuition and miscellaneous costs
5. School uniform requirements, if applicable, and approximate costs plus the availability of secondhand uniforms
6. Lunch facilities and approximate cost
7. School hours

If bringing a spouse along with you on the exchange, make sure that the person who will be spending the most time at the new home is the one to choose the home. One professor from the Massachusetts Institute of Technology exchanged with a retired couple who lived near New York University. The professor had traded primarily because of the closeness of the home to N.Y.U., but his wife was quite dissatisfied with the home, a rather small apartment. Apartment size hadn't occurred to him since he only needed a place to sleep in, but she had to spend a good deal of time in those cramped quarters.

Obviously, it's best if any dependents are actively involved in some activity while on an exchange with you. Children will be attending school classes during the school year and going back to school is also an excellent idea for many spouses who are not otherwise occupied. Then he or she can travel to the campus with you and not feel trapped in your exchange home. Ask your contact at the school or your department secretary about priority registration for faculty dependents.

Many governments will allow non-citizen spouses to work part-time to supplement your income (and in some countries lucrative but slightly less than legal employment is available for native English speakers, writers, and editors). Check first with the job placement office at the university you'll be teaching at or with the secretary or contact in your new school.

Student exchangers have priorities similar to those of teachers in considering which family to stay with: home proximity to school, transportation, and home study facilities (desk, typewriter, reading light). Students will probably have time to travel and sight-see, so comparing family inclination to travel also will be of consequence in determining choice.

Written Agreements

Exchanging involves many details. Ambiguity over who is responsible for what, what basic understanding exists, and who has what authority can result. Many swappers exchanging repeatedly merely brush aside or excuse misunderstandings and conflicts as "part of the game." That's an ideal attitude, but you can relieve yourself of the more important potential irritants by defining the exchange on paper. A written agreement between partners in effect is a restatement of promise in more concrete, binding terms.

A written agreement also validates or dismisses your assumptions. It's too easy when talking over the telephone with a fascinating person who has a confusing but intriguing accent to get lost in niceties, discussions about the weather and scenery, and all the while worrying about the long distance charges you're tallying up. No practical information gets discussed. You might feel embarrassed to ask questions when she seems such an obviously pleasant woman. A written agreement gives you a more secure feeling of what you're getting into.

ADVICE ALERT
(from Vince, Jo Ann, Andre & Ariel Botta, Bar Harbor, Maine)
"BE TRUSTING AND GENEROUS. YOUR THOUGHTFULNESS WILL BE RETURNED MANY TIMES OVER. EXCHANGE LIKE FACILITIES, I.E., PRIMARY RESIDENCES, NOT A SECOND HOME. THEN BOTH PARTIES ARE MAKING SIMILAR COMMITMENTS. IF YOU HAVE CHILDREN, EXCHANGE WITH OTHER FAMILIES. YOUR KIDS WILL FIND A BONANZA OF "NEW" TOYS AND A VERY PERSONAL VACATION."

The agreement should be kept to one page so as not to appear too intimidating. Discuss and agree on points to be covered with your partner prior to writing the agreement. Here are some points that are easily covered:

1. Behavior
2. Home and Area Information List
3. Automobiles
4. Utility and Telephone
5. Appliance and Automobile Repair
6. Mail Delivery
7. Yard Work and Home Maintenance
8. Maid Service
9. Newspaper Delivery
10. Pets
11. Designating a Primary Reference

Following is a sample agreement that covers these points. An attachment of household rules and instructions would be typed and left at each residence.

EXCHANGE AGREEMENT

1. Each party of visitors shall take good care of their temporary homes, leaving the home in the same condition that the owners left it in for them.

2. Each party shall clean and otherwise prepare their own home for their guests. A detailed Home and Area Information List shall be left for the visitors, along with home operating procedures and appliance information.

3. Automobiles will be fully insured by the owners for liability and property damage for the visitors' use. Exchanged autos must be newly tuned up and in running condition, and not obviously in need of mechanical repair. Visitors shall pay the deductible of the insurance policy for each automobile accident, if the accident is proven to be a result of their fault, except if the accident is proven to have been caused by mechanical failure, in which case the owner will pay the deductible. Visitors shall pay for gasoline and oil, and the owner will pay all repair and upkeep bills.

4. Owners will be forwarded utility and phone bills (costs of which have been accumulated by the visitors), review them, and mail the bills back to the visitors, which the visitors will then pay.

5. Visitors will make every attempt to telephone the owner in event of any forthcoming major repair (any repair estimated at over U.S. $100), for the owner to approve or disapprove. The owner is responsible for paying all repairs, unless an item is broken as a result of visitor negligence.

6. We shall both make arrangements so that all mail will be automatically rerouted by the local post office to the visitor's temporary address.

7. Each owner will prearrange for yard work and pool upkeep to be taken care of by an independent contractor (such as a weekly gardener). Owners will leave prewritten checks or cash for the visitors to pay for these services.

8. Each visitor is responsible for routine housework.

9. Each owner will prepay newspaper delivery for the duration of the exchange.

10. Each owner will leave adequate food for pets, and visitors will feed the animals on a regular basis.

11. Each owner will designate a nearby neighbor who has agreed to the duty as a Primary Reference Person for the visitors, to assist them with problems and answer questions.

Additions or deletions to this agreement must be initialed by each exchanger.

Exchanger: _____

Date: _____

Exchanger:_____

Date:_____

After you decide with your partner what points an agreement should cover, type up a draft, photocopy it once, sign both copies, and mail them to your partner. If he is satisfied with the agreement he should sign both copies, keep one, and send you the other. If he has additions or deletions to make, he should initial each change on both copies, sign them, and return both to you. Then it would be up to you to counter-initial each change and return his one copy.

Notice that the wording used is left rather vague. This is done purposely, since the written agreement is not intended to serve as the centerpiece of your understanding. Trust is. The agreement is just insurance. Notice also that the language used is not legal jargon. Difficult language will delay the agreement process and most probably scare international partners. Keep it general and simply worded.

Chapter 8

Easing Your Pre-Swap Worries

After finding a partner and agreeing to an exchange most people are filled with a flush of exuberance and wild expectation. They've done it. They're going to Milan or Quebec or wherever and they have a real house to stay in — for free.

It's time now to temper that enthusiasm with dutiful execution of responsibility. There are still plenty of details to iron out before spooning gelato and sipping espresso in a nook that time apparently forgot.

This is a chapter of details; notes and advice gleaned from many different exchangers who have learned via trial and error (many with heavy emphasis on the latter). Use this chapter in conjunction with appendix C and your partner to define the rules you'll each play by and prepare yourselves and families for a wonderful time.

Preparing To Trade Is Unique

A "normal" vacation is preceded by a generally well-known group of tasks: ask your son or daughter to take the cat or dog, get the traveler's checks, pick up the plane tickets, arrange for the neighbor to water the lawns, stop delivery of the newspaper, turn out the lights (except for the porch), and lock up. Pretty standard stuff. Home exchange preparation bears little resemblance to this pattern. There are more and different things to do.

If you haven't already, make sure that you and your partner are clear on the exchange dates and length of stay, with the international dateline in mind if applicable. More than once I've expected guests to arrive only to realize that they were not due until the following day. Try to be as accommodating as possible concerning exchange dates. It's unusual when partners want to trade for precisely the same duration. Try to remain adaptable. If vacation lengths cannot be reconciled, one party may want to consider touring a bit prior to returning home. This is common. Who would want to exchange homes with a family in Beijing without stopping in Shanghai before or after the exchange?

Your home must be cleaned before the arrival of your guests. They'll undoubtedly be cleaning their home for you. Make sure everything is in good order, from the floors and carpets to the outside lawns and gardens. Think of it as if you were preparing to throw a large party, except that the job really has to be a little more extensive since your exchangers will be using the home as you normally do, to sleep, shower, cook, and live in. All towels, linens, and bed sheets should be freshly washed. Some exchangers I've talked with will clean the home inside and out and leave for the exchange, whereupon a cleaning service they've hired will come in and give the floors, carpets, and furniture a final going over. Just make sure the cleaning is done prior to your exchangers arriving.

It's not worth worrying about cherished items and heirlooms. Store them somewhere. The presence of delicate vases or breakable objects might only scare and inhibit guests in your home anyway, especially if small children are coming on the exchange. Remember there is a danger with removing too many things, since it can leave your home devoid of character and make the experience less insightful for your guests. It's important for them and likewise yourself to see and understand what styles of art people in other parts of the world collect and how they design their living spaces. This is part of the culture that swapping homes reveals. Don't worry, chances are very good that they will take painstaking care of your belongings.

Your exchangers, like you, will be taking a fair amount of baggage packed with underclothes, shirts, blouses, pants, skirts, and coats. Accordingly, leave them plenty of empty closet space with hangers and barren dresser drawers. Remove all your belongings from desk drawers in the study and by the telephone, where they may want to put things of their own. Kitchen drawers and cabinets should be left full of utensils, pots and pans, and assorted kitchen cleaning liquids and tools. Remember to move toxic substances from under the sink if small children will be coming to stay, have such bottles marked and do the same with dangerous compounds in the garage.

It's a wise idea to have three copies of house keys and two of car keys available for your partners. Leave them the car keys and two sets of the house keys, with the third set left with their designated primary reference person. Both of you then can, if needed, pick up keys with someone when you arrive at the homes. But, it is more convenient and pleasant to meet at one destination or the other and exchange keys, or trade keys at an intermediate airport. Barring a meeting it is vastly preferable for your primary reference person to meet the family at the local airport, drive them home, and let them in.

It is always an aim of exchangers to make the other party feel comfortable in their temporary home, and besides having the home clean it is inviting to have a "welcome home" gift awaiting your tired guests. Anything from chilled champagne, baked cookies or chocolates to major league baseball or concert tickets would be appreciated. That will set their vacation off on a high note.

Though generosity is admirable there are undoubtedly consumable items in the home that you don't want consumed. Canned goods, homemade jams and pickles, liquor and wine can all be left in place as long as you let your partner know that they're not to be used, and mark them so. Make sure that you and your family likewise understand what it is in their home that is "off-limits."

Recreation and sporting equipment usage also needs to be defined. Can your partner's children use your kid's baseball mitts, balls and bats? What about your golf cart and your husband's clubs? Bicycles? Snowmobiles and off-road motorcycles? Toys, boats, fishing gear? Most exchangers do trade all of these things, with assistance and guidance from neighbors where appropriate.

It is possible to arrange for mail to be delivered to your new home if the exchange will be a lengthy one since most of us have bills and checks interspersed in with the daily stack of junk mail. If you would prefer that the post office not hold or deliver the mail to your permanent address, ask your local post office if they will automatically re-route personally addressed letters to your temporary home.

They usually will (while sorting out and not forwarding the junk). Be sure to tell them when to stop forwarding your mail — a couple of weeks prior to your return from distant locations — or your exchangers will be sending it back to you. Packages, because of the cost to forward them, can be sent through to your normal address. On shorter exchanges of two to four weeks it works out better to just let the mail accumulate at home. Very important mail can be sent quicker to you by arranging with your partner to look for a certain return address, and then slipping the letter into a prepaid, pre-addressed express mail envelope.

Day to day upkeep must be clarified too, such as garbage pick-up days, separation of recycled materials like newspaper, glass, and aluminum and whether leaves will be picked up along with garbage or separately.

Insurance, Money, And Automobiles

As a rule, standard homeowner's insurance policies will insure your partners in your home since they are your guests and are staying for free. If compensation is being paid, insurance companies are likely to view guests as renters; thus additional coverage will be needed to cover you against theft, vandalism, breakage, fire. Duration of the exchange also may matter to your insurance agent. Longer stays by exchange partners may not be fully covered. Check with your agent. Home insurance during an exchange costs extra in some European countries, so if swapping to Europe your partner may be paying this extra fee.

You also must check with your car insurance agent to make sure that others driving your vehicles will be insured in a comprehensive manner for collision, mechanical failure, theft, and vandalism. Some sort of towing service also is a must, and you may have to apply for this on your partner's behalf through your insurance company.

Health and medical insurance also demands a bit of investigation. The majority of insurance companies offering health insurance in the U.S. extend coverage for international vacations. Some limit coverage to the contiguous states. Some foreign insurance providers also extend their policies to cover policy holders abroad. Not to fret if you're left out in the cold, however, since short-term international medical coverage can be purchased at travel agencies and many banks that offer traveler's checks, where you can simply pay an extra $5 for medical coverage. If your exchange partners don't have international medical coverage and for some reason can't get it, they can go to a travel agency near your home and purchase short-term coverage. Regardless of whether you are covered by a firm in your home country or not, it can be advantageous to buy additional insurance in countries with national health insurance. Ask your partners if their government offers inexpensive policies. Nationalized coverage is preferable since you typically prepay on a monthly basis and won't be required to pay full costs in cash and then bill your insurance company back home. That can take forever and be more trouble than it's worth if the charge is minor.

Travel agencies sell trip cancellation insurance that covers all prepaid expenses that you can document with receipts, at a cost of approximately $4 to $5 per $100 of your paid expenses.

Both INTERVAC International and the Directory Group Association are planning to offer subscribers "exchange insurance," to guard against the possibility of one partner backing out of an exchange agreement just before flights leave. Insurance would most probably cover home damage as well.

Most exchangers resolve the question of what form of money to take by bringing traveler's checks, a credit card or two, and a small amount of cash. Depending on which country you're going to this can prove expensive, especially if you'll be cashing traveler's checks or using credit cards in less populated areas where shop keepers routinely take 5 to 10 percent extra "for their trouble." Using dollar denominations frequently meets the same end, that of costing you a hefty surcharge. This can happen in metropolitan areas as well if you exchange traveler's checks or dollars in hotels or small banks that don't reflect the actual currency exchange rate.

ADVICE ALERT
(from Hazel Nayar, Derby, England)
"YOU MUST RELAX. MANY PEOPLE FREAK OUT CLEANING UP AND PREPARING."

There is a way to get around paying any bank commissions or surcharges. Exchangers, with the assistance of each other before the exchange, can open interest-paying bank or postal accounts in the country they'll be visiting, using their partner's money. Here's how it works. Partners agree on a sum that approximates what each would be bringing with them on the exchange, say, U.S. $1,500.00. Each partner then deposits this amount of his own money in a local bank account opened in his partner's name. In the U.S., accounts can typically be opened simply by sending the coming exchanger two signature cards to sign, which he then returns to his U.S. partner who takes the cards to the bank and deposits $1,500.00 of his own money. That same day the other partner can do the same, using the currency exchange rate given in the *Wall Street Journal*. Receipts of deposit should then be mailed to each other or exchanged upon meeting, along with settling exact amounts deposited. The process varies somewhat country to country, but it is generally possible. In England the visiting exchanger must be present to open a checking account, but the departing exchanger can deposit the amount to be credited (a letter of credit) to the account when it opens. In Austria, Japan, and other countries, interest-bearing postal accounts can be opened and funds deposited with ease by your partner in your name. Such postal accounts are usually far more convenient than bank accounts, having more branch offices, shorter waits, and sometimes longer hours. This system is particularly useful for exchangers coming from countries where the amount of cash for export is limited; in this case only pocket money is needed until you arrive at your temporary home and pick up your bank or postal book. Then you'll have all your money with you, in that country's currency, and all without having paid a cent for the exchange of money.

Automobiles are another matter of ample concern. Your car should be newly tuned up and have a full tank of gasoline. If the vehicle burns oil, make sure your partner knows it. Have several extra quarts of oil on hand. The car should be clean and waxed if possible on the outside and vacuumed inside. Make sure the trunk contains all desirable emergency road equipment: flares, spare tire, tools and jack, flashlight, and first aid kit. Copies of road maps and a paper listing the emergency road service telephone number are thoughtful ideas.

If you plan to drive in a foreign country it's advisable to purchase an International Driver's License from your local American Automobile Association office. This is not required of visiting drivers in all countries, but showing the card — which has a translation of your license in the appropriate language — can make it easier to rent a car and placate traffic officers. Cost is approximately $5.

You may want to set an upper mileage limit on how many miles each of you may drive each other's automobiles. It is not uncommon for Americans or Canadians returning to their homes to find that their partners drove their car in North America considerably further than the Americans or Canadians drove their partner's auto abroad. Remember that long distance mass transit isn't well developed in North America, and we live in large countries where long distances seem shorter. Asian and European countries typically are smaller, boast better mass transit, but suffer from higher fuel costs. Thus the frequent imbalance in miles driven on transatlantic and transpacific exchanges. Nevertheless, this can take a toll on your car. Figure out where you think they'll want to go, add up the approximate mileage, and suggest a realistic yet gracious mileage limit. Past that, they might agree to pay a per mile charge of 15 cents.

For long-term stays in Great Britain when an auto is not included as part of the exchange, there are automotive dealers who will sell you a new or used car and guarantee to buy the vehicle back when you are finished at a fixed price. This is usually less expensive than renting. Write the British Tourist Authority, Thames Tower, Black's Road, London W6 9EL for dealer addresses.

Yard Work, Bills, Deliveries, And Pets

These are just a few more suggestions to make your home easier to care for while you're away and easier to readjust to once you return. Your partners, just like you at their home, will be either vacationing or preoccupied working; therefore duties like yard work and caring for pets should be kept to a minimum unless your exchange partners specify that they don't mind doing these things. In general, yard work, gardening, plant care, and lawn mowing are best left to a paid gardener or to neighbors. Many exchangers will perform these tasks but chances are they would rather see the Grand Canyon than mow your lawn (and wouldn't you really rather that they do see the Grand Canyon?). Besides, if they aren't doing these things for you, you probably will not have to do them at your temporary home, either. The same logic applies for pool service, cleaning help, and pet care. The consideration, of course, is that having these things done will cost both partners. It matters on how much money you can jointly afford, how much free time you each plan on having at each other's home, and how large the homes and grounds are.

Pets are somewhat an exception. There can be no dispute that pets are happiest and most comfortable at their home. I've had exchangers comment that their pets seemed healthy and at ease after being left at their normal home under the charge of exchange guests, whereas the pets are emotional wrecks if they are left in unfamiliar surroundings with friends or relatives. Especially if your partners are bringing children, they probably won't mind caring for your pets. (The children may whine if they don't get to care for your pets.)

Unusual or special pets are another story. I'm not sure if a pet boa constrictor would really notice if you weren't around for a couple of months. If a pet requires difficult care you're best to find someone who you can personally verse on proper care prior to leaving.

ADVICE ALERT
(from Ellie and Jim Chastain, Washington, D.C.)
"LEAVE BREAKFAST STUFF FOR THEIR FIRST DAY AND A NOTE TELLING THEM TO HELP THEMSELVES. MAKE SURE TO TREAT YOUR EXCHANGER LIKE A FRIEND!"

Try to anticipate any deliveries you will have coming while on vacation and leave cash to pay for them, if necessary. Pre-pay as much as possible, from deliveries to house services such as gardeners to routine bills such as garbage pickup. Typically you will have some things to ask your exchanger to do and some duties that you will pre-pay to have done, while your partner will have different things for you to do while paying for different services for you. Don't hesitate to suggest that care for something of your partner's (the dog, cat, and chickens) be traded for duties at your home (watering the indoor plants, gardens, and lawns). That's a good way to save money.

How To Make Life Easier For Your Partner And Yourself

As you can see, there are many actions you can take to help your exchange partner while his family stays in your home. Conversely, don't forget to ask that your partner be preparing with the same concern for you and your family.

Perhaps the single most important thing you can do to assist your partner is to designate a primary reference person for your guest family. Make it clear to the person what is required: he may have to pick the family up at the airport, show them around your home and explain quirky appliances, drive them around the local area to explain logistically where they are, perhaps offer to take them to some community activities and host a "neighborhood party" for them, and be prepared to answer lots of questions. You might also tell him that he'll get a valuable opportunity that you won't: to meet and intimately befriend a visiting family.

In order for your primary reference person to be most helpful to your guests, you'll have to show him around your house, pointing out special appliance directions, burglar alarms, electric garage door operation, gas and electricity meters and fuse box location, lighting, smoke detector, fire extinguisher, and how to start up and operate your car(s). All of these things should also be typed on pages and bound with your completed photocopy of appendix C for your partner's reference.

Ask your partner what kind of foods his family normally eats so that you can buy and leave enough food and drink in the refrigerator for a day or two. If you're not sure what they like, go with the staples: milk, beer, soft drinks, bread, chicken or fish, cheese, butter, eggs, fruit, and vegetables.

Two monthly bills that are typically not pre-paid are telephone and utility charges since uses can vary greatly between partners. The easiest method for telephone bills is to have visitors pay the entire bill or only for the long-distance calls, with owners picking up the local charges. Bills can be sent back and forth, but this isn't really necessary as long as users keep track of each long-distance call by dialing the operator immediately after each long-distance call and requesting the amount of the call, which should then be kept on a tally near the phone. Upon leaving each other's home, visitors then leave enough cash to cover those calls. Utilities, because of sometimes exorbitant heating and air conditioning costs, should be paid in full by users. To pay the last month's bill, you can either estimate by leaving cash to cover an amount equal to last month's bill or agree ahead of time to settle last month charges after the exchange.

Leave your partner duplicates of the maps and tourist brochures that you sent them in the mail prior to agreeing to the swap in case they forgot to bring those guides with them.

Your exchange family's first day in your area is very important to their overall impression of the vacation. They will be tired if coming off of a long flight and quite possibly hungry. If you will not be meeting them in your own area, instruct the primary reference person to pick them up at the airport and take them straight home. A low-key home cooked meal would be fantastic, but fast food of decent quality will serve the purpose quicker and less obtrusively. They may say they feel fine but privately feel like eating and resting alone. Above all, recommend that your primary reference person not plan a welcoming party, however well intended, for the first night they arrive.

One of the things that experienced exchangers regret most often is not having met former exchange partners who they have written and talked with over the telephone. If at all possible, try to arrange a meeting either at one of the destinations by one party arriving one day early, or at an intermediate airport that you'll both be flying through. Besides getting to know one another in person and feeling better about your home's security, you'll gain valuable insight into the personalities that created the home you'll be staying in, as well as have a convenient way to clear up any ambiguous points, exchange keys and bank books (if you deposited money in accounts for each other), and remember any last minute details that you've forgotten to explain in the previous few months. If you'll be welcoming the exchange family to your home before departing yourself and can afford to, it's a nice idea to rent a hotel room for yourself and family near your home so that your guests can spend their first, exhausted night alone in your home. Now that's thoughtful.

Chapter 9

Enjoying Your Exchange

Just as there is preparation and precaution that can relieve pre-swap headaches, there are also specific ideas and actions to keep in mind that can make your vacation more carefree and help you to fully appreciate your new home, neighbors, and the area you are in. There will be fascinating places to go and marvelous things to see. This is to help you make the most of it.

Caring For Your Partner's Home

Vital during your stay at your partner's home is a respect for the property. Most exchangers take meticulous care of their temporary homes, in many ways better care than they take of their own homes. This isn't surprising considering the general feeling of indebtedness and slight apprehension that swappers on vacation typically exhibit, no doubt due to the relationship built up between the homeowners proceeding the switch. It's a special relationship, different from a normal friendship since exchangers have been dealing with one another from long distances, their agreement resting on a foundation of fragile trust. Partners are conscious about upholding their portion of the bargain, reasoning that if they act responsibly their partners will do likewise. Consequently, your home is probably more at risk with best friends staying there than if exchange partners are inhabiting the premises. Old friends will take liberties with your property that exchangers wouldn't dare take. It is this conscientious behavior that you should duplicate in your exchanger's home.

Your partner's neighbors and relatives will likely prove your greatest asset throughout your stay, so it's a good idea to remember them prior to leaving your own home by packing along representative small gifts from your area to present to them when you meet. While living in Japan I found the Japanese to be especially prolific gift givers. *Omiyage* (small gifts) are liberally dispensed when visiting someone's house or given to members of one's family upon returning from a trip, taking the shape of candies, flowers, cookies, and the like. Small tokens such as these are a worthwhile investment in any country, often counting disproportionately towards the creation of a friendly ambience.

Soon after arriving at your partner's home, make a physical check along with the household instruction booklet that should be left for you to make sure that everything is being covered, either being taken care of by you, a neighbor, or a paid service. If something surprises and perplexes you, check first with your primary reference source, then telephone your partner if the situation is still not being taken care of to your satisfaction (or to your perception of your partner's satisfaction).

Similarly, you'll have to do a mental check on duty responsibility if after being at the home for a while you plan on prolonged touring. Make sure that all of the duties that you or members of your family are in charge of are transferred to neighbors or a paid service who are aware of their new responsibility. Before leaving your temporary home for days or weeks at a time, it's a good idea to get your new neighbor's telephone numbers in case you run into problems while touring and need advice. Calling the primary reference person once every week or so just to make sure the exchangers at your home haven't called with a pressing message for you also is recommended. Inform the reference person ahead of time that you may be calling for this reason.

If while staying at your partner's home an object is broken by someone in your family and it does not appear repairable, you should be willing to pay for replacement of the item. Before leaving the money for your partner, however, telephone him to make sure the object does not just habitually break. Something that you apparently broke or ruined may have in reality been no good prior to your arrival. He may laugh and apologize for not warning you. Or he may decide that he can fix it. It's worth a call.

Most damage will be repairable. Try to objectively ascertain whether the damage was strictly a result of your use, or whether the damage was a cumulative result of use by your partner's family and yours. If the item isn't expensive to fix you may just want to go ahead and pay for it, but some repairs, particularly automotive, will be costly. Moreover, typical vehicle problems are cumulative in nature, so the owner should share in repair cost. Most exchangers agree that minor repair bills can be initiated by the guest and charged to the owner, but that bills over a certain amount must first be cleared by the owner over the telephone before the repair can be made. (This should be covered in your written agreement.) Repair of such appliances as stereos and kitchen ovens will most times fit in this category. Neighbors can be a helpful source of advice when you're trying to figure out how expensive something will be to fix. They can usually assist you in taking the unit in to an appropriate but not over-priced repair shop or calling a repair person for you.

You'll probably have to answer a fair number of telephone calls and people at the door inquiring about the owner's whereabouts. This won't be a problem unless you are less than fluent in the language being spoken. You might be able to use English in reply to a different language, hoping for a bilingual inquirer, but it helps if you can string a few basic words together to offer a partial explanation of where your partners are. The following will usually suffice: "Hello. Mr. and Mrs. — are not at home. They will return on —." If the person at the door or on the phone seems to persist by asking another question, use this reply: "I'm sorry, I don't speak —. Do you speak —?" Upon hearing this most people will either answer in the language you specified, hang up or smile and walk away.

ADVICE ALERT
(from Kay McFarland, Port Orange, Florida)
"FIND OUT IF INTERIOR OF HOME IS COMFORTABLE. I JUST RETURNED FROM THE ONLY EXCHANGE I'VE EVER HAD THAT WAS UNSATISFACTORY. NO EASY CHAIRS, NO READING LIGHTS (I RIGGED UP A "TROUBLE LIGHT" I FOUND IN HIS GARAGE), NO DRYER. THE TV ONLY GOT ONE CHANNEL — POORLY! NOTHING LIKE MY BEST EXCHANGE IN SCOTLAND. NOW I HAVE A QUESTIONNAIRE I WILL USE IN FUTURE EXCHANGES."

Hospitality Exchanging

Hospitality exchanging— essentially sleep quarters' swapping— requires a special attitude on your part so you can interact well with your adopted family. You'll benefit from having an experienced family who can answer questions and give you advice. At the best, you'll make close, intimate friends and be treated as a member of a foreign family.

Hospitality exchanging is rightfully renown as the ultimate situation for serious foreign language study. There's no quicker way to learn the language than to go to school or work and then return home to a native speaking family with whom you must live and communicate. Often times that family will expect you to willingly act as a language tutor for them, a task that can consume a great deal of time and be quite boring. Yet this may be what's required to make you a "part of the family," and to refuse to offer help might sour your budding relationship before it has a chance to flower. Make it clear at the beginning that one of your main goals is to speak their language as much as possible, but be sensitive to special needs of the family. Does the father need to improve his English for business reasons? Are the kids studying your language in school? Eat their foods, speak their language, and practice their customs, but offering assistance in such circumstances will earn you a contributory role in the family that can't be erased.

If you will be coming as a student in a youth hospitality exchange, ask your exchange partner to send you a map and photographs of the campus, along with telephone numbers of students who will be able to give you an informal orientation at the school. It helps greatly if your friends at home can do the same for your partner upon his arrival, welcoming him into your group of friends. An instant support group of fellow students can relieve much of the stress and insecurity felt by exchange students in thier new environment.

You will represent more than yourself in the eyes of your new family, classmates, and acquaintances. Your personality and behavior will be generalized to your whole home country.

Searching Out Those Local Favorites

Whether you will be vacationing or working while on your exchange, you enter into a situation complete with the built-in support network of your partner's relatives and friends. This has considerable advantage over staying in a typical tourist accommodation for gaining a deep understanding of the area and people you're visiting.

For the most part, the patterns of transportation and daily living that people in your new community follow are considerably different from the rehearsed pattern that tourists are ushered through on short stays. Tourists are deprived of the less glamorous routine local lifestyle, though certainly not by happenstance since this is exactly what many of them are trying to avoid. But of course it is this very avoidance that leaves most tourists with a superficial knowledge at best of the places they've visited. Your "adopted" neighbors and relatives are your link to crossing over into the lives of everyday people and living as they do. Understanding by experience.

To cultivate these relationships, ask frequent questions and invite them to accompany you on brief sojourns around the area. Not only will they save you time and keep you from getting lost, they also will begin to suggest how you should spend your time in the area. Many persons, prideful of their home town, will expect you to see the local points of tourist interest. Oblige them and see these places first. Then begin questioning them on where they go and what they do for recreation, dining, relaxation. Answers will probably be modest: the local park, a small but fun pizza parlor, perhaps a back yard barbecue, but these are the activities at which you'll get a true feeling of community, one where you can see residents at ease in their environment. You'll also have terrific fun.

You will find that the amount of money spent when out with your partner's friends and relatives has no correlation with enjoyment and honest companionship. Even if you swap into a different social and economic strata, the informal gatherings and parties are likely to leave the most memorable impressions compared to the cruises, five-star restaurants, and castles. Let your new neighbors and relatives know that you want to do the things with them that they normally do. Don't let them go out of their way too much on your account. That kind of involvement will lead to acceptance and long-term friendship which, after all, is what home exchanging is all about. "I feel sorry for Jesse and Nilda in a way," a neighbor of the long time home exchangers told me. "We had the pleasure to meet and take care of people from Belgium, Mexico, Italy, and New Zealand. They were all great people, but just normal, like you and me. That's the way we treated them, and I think that's the way they wanted to be treated."

Exchangers are seen as ambassadors representing their home country, state, or province by natives in the area they are visiting. It seems that nothing impresses people more — good or bad — than personal contact with foreigners. The positive impression a Paris woman gets after having lunch with a polite, sincere, honest man from Texas will erase the dishonest images she absorbs from watching television. You as an exchanger have a unique chance to represent your own community to the world, to dissolve old stereotypes perpetuated by the mass media, ethnic jokes, bigotry, and ignorance.

ADVICE ALERT
(from Charles R. Yarbrough, Wahiawa, Hawaii)
"AN EXCELLENT WAY TO TRAVEL. SUPER. RECOMMEND A STAY OF AT LEAST FOUR WEEKS IN ORDER TO FULLY APPRECIATE AND ENJOY YOUR SURROUNDINGS. HAVE FUN!"

Author's Note

Home exchangers comprise a surprisingly large network of travelers, but one that is conspicuously interpersonal and private in nature. We find out about each other largely through contact together or through intermediaries, commonly friends and business acquaintances.

A network with these attributes is not very efficient in the rapid dissemination of information. It's difficult for us as home exchangers to share information that can make exchanging better, easier and more gratifying.

Perhaps this book can serve that function of spreading home exchange ideas and suggestions quicker. If you find inadequacies and/or mistakes in this edition or, just as importantly, have time-proven advice of your own that you would like to share with other home exchangers, write me in care of The East Woods Press, 429 East Boulevard, Charlotte, North Carolina 28203, U.S.A., so that I may amend *Home Exchanging* with your ideas.

Through your input our network can grow stronger. Each revised edition of this book can then serve as our common meeting ground for the refinement and advancement of the home exchanging process.

Jim Dearing
Los Angeles, California
1985

Appendix A

General Information

This Appendix lists home exchange agencies, United States governmental services and educational exchange organizations, other exchange organizations not easily classifiable, some reference sources for exchangers, and a few translation services.

Should you join an exchange agency and, if so, which one? You can come to your own conclusion about the first question by reading the appropriate sections of chapters 4 and 5. Deciding which agency will turn up the most and best offers in response to your offer is more difficult to ascertain, though it isn't necessarily that important of a decision. Most annual fees are nominal — the price of a year-long magazine subscription. There are no taboos about joining more than one agency (or switching competitive catalogs with a friend). The four primary considerations are: Is this company reputable (how long have they been in the home exchange listing business)? From which geographic areas are the majority of their listings (and are these the areas that you want to go to)? How many subscribers do they have? Is there a sense of balance in their offerings (does supply equal demand) or do they have too many subscribers from your area which would make the chance of finding a good partner unlikely? These issues are all interrelated. A huge but poorly-balanced agency is of little practical use, just as is a smaller "boutique" agency that will fold in six months. Either in writing or over the telephone, ask them the aforementioned four questions and make your decision accordingly.

Affiliated exchange agencies such as the Directory Group Association and INTERVAC International prefer that interested persons join the agency affiliate in their own country — agencies in each respective group receive the same catalog for their memberships anyway. If there isn't a home exchange agency listed in your home country, join a firm in a nearby country that lists subscribers in the country you want to travel to, or join an agency based in the country that you intend to visit.

The governmental services and educational exchange organizations can sometimes be of assistance if you are exchanging for business, governmental, or educational purposes.

The other exchange organizations listed are each committed in slightly different ways to the promotion of cultural understanding, issue awareness and world peace. Participants must demonstrate these values to be welcomed into one of these programs.

The reference sources for exchangers are included as a supplement to appendix B except for the two cultural handbooks listed from Intercultural Press, Inc. If you want to stay in a country not represented in appendix B or need additional newspaper and school addresses in the listed countries, your local library will be able to provide at least several of these reference books for your perusal.

HOME EXCHANGE AGENCIES

AUSTRALIA
Holiday Home Exchange, Suite 10 Mona Vale Plaza, Bungan Street, Mona Vale 2103, N.S.W., Australia. Tele: 02 997-7000. Subscribers of this relatively small agency benefit by receiving the Directory Group Association Exchange Book with approximately 6000 listings.

AUSTRIA
INTERVAC Austria, Amselweg 4, A-9100 Volkermarkt, Austria. Tele: 42 32 2147.

BELGIUM
INTERVAC Belgium, Bodegem Straat 148a, 1740 Ternat, Belgium. Tele: 2 582 2266. Subscribers of this small to moderate size agency receive the 4000-listing INTERVAC Catalog.

BRAZIL
INTERVAC Brazil, Rua Nascimento Silva, 126-Apto 501, Epenema, Rio de Janeiro, Brazil. The newest INTERVAC member. If the organizer acts aggressively this could open up a whole new market for INTERVAC subscribers.

CANADA
Canadian Exchange Club, R.R. 3, Collingwood, Ontario, L9Y 322, Canada. Tele: 705 445-5070. Affiliate member of the Directory Group Associaton.

DENMARK
Dansk International Bolig Udveksling, Rontoftevej 27, DK-2860 Soborg, Denmark. Tele: 1-562014. DGA affiliate.
INTERVAC Denmark, Boite Postale 3, L-8201 G.D. Luxembourg. Tele: 352 3107 24.

ENGLAND

AIJ-Amitie International Des Jeunes, Beaver House, 1oa Woodborough Road, London SW15 6QA, England. Tele: 01-788 6857. Arranges exchanges between individuals in England and France.

Euro Vacation Exchange, New Barn House, Toft Road, Kingston, Cambridgeshire CB3 7NS, England. Tele: 022026 2783. Your advertisement is circulated to subscribers throughout Western Europe free of charge. If you find an exchange partner the agency will bill you U.S. $50. Their strengths are in Western Europe, Denmark, France, and Holland, with some subscribers in Germany, Italy, Spain, and the U.S.

Holiday-80, 43 Hampton Road, Forest Gate, London E7 OPD, England. Tele: 01-534 2723, 01-681 6866. This is an agency for European teachers in 17 different countries. Only union instructors are listed.

Home Interchange Ltd., 8 Hillside, Farningham — Kent DA4 ODD, England. Tele: 0322 86 4527. One of the largest members of the Directory Group Association, with over 800 Great Britain listings.

INTERVAC Great Britain, 6 Siddals Land, Allestree, Berby DE 3 2DY, England. Tele: 0332 55 8931. One of INTERVAC's largest members with over 600 listings. The organizer has begun regular public meetings to help promote home exchanging and bring members together to share ideas.

Worldwide Home Exchange Club, 139a Sloane Street, London SWI. Tele: 01 589 6055. Publishes 2 listings with primarily European subscribers.

FINLAND

INTERVAC Finland, Kellosilta 7, SF 00520 Helsinki 52, Finland. Tele: 0 150 2484.

FRANCE

INTERVAC France, 55 rue Nationale, F 37000 Tours, France. Tele: 47 202057. Largest INTERVAC affiliate.

Sejours, Les Sycomores des Logissons, F-13770 Venelles, France. Tele: 42 610557. DGA affiliate.

Appendix A 123

IRELAND

Holiday-80, Rusheen, Clanricarde, Boreenmanna Road, Cork, Ireland. Open to union teachers in 17 countries including the United States. Swaps arranged by Holiday-80 in Ireland. No catalog is offered. Holiday-80 has 200 subscribers in Ireland alone. Cost is approximately $7 to register and $50 when an exchange is agreed upon.

Holiday Exchange International, 95 Bracken Drive, Portmarnock, Co. Dublin, Ireland. Tele: 1 462598. DGA affiliate.

INTERVAC Ireland, Phillipstown, Ballymakenny Road, Drogheda, Ireland. Tele: 041 3 7969.

ISRAEL

INTERVAC Israel, P.O. Box 2045, Herzliya, 46103, Israel.

ITALY

Home Vacation — Casa Vacance, Piazza de Gasperi 41, 1-35100 Padova, Italy. Tele: 49 38664. DGA affiliate.

INTERVAC Italy, Via Oreglia 18, 4004, Riola di Vergato (Bologna). Tele: 051 910818.

LUXEMBOURG

INTERVAC Luxembourg, Boite Postale 3, L-8201 G.D. Luxembourg. Tele: 352 310724.

NETHERLANDS

Home to Home Holidays, P.O. Box 279, 1900 AG Castricum, Netherlands. Tele: 025185 7953. Includes rentals along with exchanges. Austria, Britain, Wales, Czechoslovakia, Denmark, France, Germany, Italy, Spain, Sweden, Switzerland, U.S., Antilles and Morocco, with a particularly large number of listings from Holland. Specify which language you want your catalog in when subscribing.

INTERVAC Netherlands, Paasberg 25, 6862 CB Oosterbeek, Netherlands. Tele: 085 341187. A very strong affiliate for INTERVAC with over 450 listings.

L.O.V.W., Pb. 412, NL-9200 AK Drachten, Netherlands. Tele: 05120 20818. DGA affiliate.

NEW ZEALAND

Holiday Home Exchange, Suite 10, Mona Vale Plaza, Bungan Street, Mona Vale 2103, N.S.W., Australia. Tele: 02 997 7000.

NORWAY

INTERVAC Norway, Fagerlivagen 9, N 2800 Gjovik, Norway. Tele: 61 73795.

PORTUGAL

Intercambio De Casas, Apdo de Correos 46315 Madrid 3, Spain. Tele: 1 4487311. DGA affiliate.

INTERVAC Spain, Mallorca 115-123, Barcelona 36, Spain. Tele: 3 254 2214.

SOUTH AFRICA

International Home Exchange, P.O. Box 188, Claremont, Cape Town 7735, South Africa. Tele: 21 666177. DGA affiliate.

SPAIN

Academic Year in Spain, Apto. 46315, Madrid, Spain. This is a program for foreign students to exchange hospitality with a Spanish student, and study at the University of Madrid.

Intercambio De Casas, Apdo de Correos 46315, Madrid 3, Spain. Tele: 1 4487311. DGA affiliate.

INTERVAC Spain, Mallorca 115-123, Barcelona 36, Spain. Tele: 3 254 2214.

SWEDEN

INTERVAC Sweden, Box 33, 55112 Jonkoping, Sweden. Tele: 036 12 82 05. If you want to go to Sweden, join INTERVAC: This agency contributes 200 subscribers who want to exchange homes. Price is reasonable.

SWITZERLAND

INTERVAC Switzerland-Liechtenstein, Reherstr, 6a, CH-9016 St. Gallen, Switzerland. Tele: 071 24 50 39. This old INTERVAC affiliate has 150 listings from Swiss exchangers, more than any other agency can boast. Prices are reasonable.

UNITED STATES OF AMERICA

Educator's Vacation Alternatives, 317 Piedmont Road, Santa Barbara, CA 93105. Tele: 805 698-2947. Main catalog published in June with fall supplement. Sixty-four page catalog is evenly divided between exchange and bed and breakfast advertisers. Listings are open to retired and active educators only, and most are in the U.S.

Exchange Network, P.O. Box 752 Ocean Springs, MS 39564. Tele: 800 562-6529. Designed for time-share property owners to exchange vacation time allotments, but home exchangers can list their homes and participate. One-time application fee is $50; match fee is $45 if printed catalog is used or $65 if you call in your request to the computerized data bank. Annual printed catalog with quarterly supplements is $47.70. Has 25,000 computerized listings worldwide, most of which are individuals wanting to exchange time-share properties. Reports 85 percent satisfaction from previous users.

Faculty Exchange Center (see entry under Government Services and Educational Organizations Offering Home or Hospitality Exchanges)

Global Home Exchange Service, Box 2015, South Burlington, VT 05401-2015. Tele: 802 985-3825. This agency goes further than most, matching families and inspecting homes, but a registration fee of $25 is required along with $175 for agreed domestic exchanges, and a registration fee of $30 with $220 closing fee for international trades.

Hawaii Home Interchange, 6398 Lake Shore Drive, San Diego, CA 92119. This small agency is a member of the Directory Group Association along with the Vacation Exchange Club. Subscribers get the DGA Exchange Book.

Hideaways International, Box 1459, Concord, MA 01742. Tele: 617 369-0252 or toll-free 1 800 843-4433 if outside Massachusetts. Publishes 3 directories and 4 supplements annually that include some exchange offers. Yearly price is $49.

Holiday Exchanges, Box 5294, Ventura, CA 93003. Tele: 805 642-4879. Publishes a monthly list of rental and exchange offers from the U.S., Great Britain, Australia, and New Zealand, with 200 to 300 annual subscribers. Yearly subscriptions are $25; renewals $18.

Home Exchange International, 185 Park Row, Suite 14D, New York, NY 10038. Tele: 212 349-5340. Western states and Mexico office: 22458 Ventura Blvd., Suite E, Woodland Hills, CA 91364-1581.

Tele: 818 992-8990. A full service agency, charging a one-time registration fee of $30 and a closing fee of $150 to $525 to find you a partner depending on type, location, and period of the exchange.

International Home Exchange Service, P.O. Box 3975, San Francisco, CA 94119. Tele: 415 382-0300. Affiliate of INTERVAC, has over 500 U.S. listings and distributes the main INTERVAC directory at the end of January, with supplements coming out at the ends of March and May. Total listings are more than 4,000. To list your home costs $45 plus shipping per year. A subscription without listing your home is $60. Twenty percent discount for subscribers over 65 years of age.

International Home Exchange Service of Hawaii, 1541 S. Beretania St., Suite 206, Honolulu, HI 96822. Tele: 808 988-6634. A branch of the San Francisco-based International Home Exchange Service.

The International Spare Room, Box 518, Solana Beach, CA 92075. Hospitality exchanges with families are offered.

InterService Home Exchange, Box 87, Glen Echo, MD 20812. Tele: 301 299-7442. Lists rentals as well as about 1,000 exchange offers, with most in the U.S., France, and England. Their main catalog is published in February with a supplement in April, both of which are very easy to read. Annual subscription with listing is $24; subscription only is $18. Fees are refundable at any time.

Interval International, 7000 S.W. 62nd Ave., Suite 306, South Miami, FL 33143. Tele: 305 666-1861. Large computerized network for resort time-share owners. Resorts must belong to Interval International for individual owners to make contacts through the network.

Loan-A-Home, 2 Park Lane 6E, Mount Vernon, NY 10552. Tele: 914 664-7640. Primarily for business people and educators who need long-term exchanges. Approximately 500 listings worldwide. There is no charge for listing your home so that others may see it. Directories are published in June and December with supplements in September and March. Cost is $20 for one directory and its supplement or $30 for all 4 publications.

Resort Condominiums International, P.O. Box 80229, Indianapolis, IN 46280-0229. Tele: 317 846-4724. Largest property exchange network in the world. Use is restricted to those individuals owning resort time-share properties in resorts registered with Resort Condominiums International. Approximately 1,000 resorts are members of RCI.

Traveler's Directory, 6224 Baynton St., Philadelphia, PA 19144. Lists 800 persons in different countries willing to provide hospitality in exchange for hospitality at a later date. Catalog is $15 and is only available to those listed.

Vacation Exchange Club, 12006 111th Ave., Unit 12, Youngtown, AZ 85363. Tele: 602 972-2186. World's largest home exchange agency with approximately 3,500 listings of its own; member of DGA; sends subscribers 6,000-listing DGA Exchange Book. Main catalog sent in February with spring supplement. Annual subscription is $22.70 with listing; catalog without listing is $15.

WorldWide Exchange, Box 1563, San Leandro, CA 94577. Tele: 415 521-7890. Publishes 4 directories per year, each with about 500 exchange offers, 80 percent of which are in the U.S. Cost is $19.95 per directory with your listing; $9.95 for 1 catalog only. Those with home or office computers and a telephone modem can access WorldWide Exchange listings on the CompuServe Travel Menu (GOWWX), which is advantageous over receiving the printed book since the computer list is updated biweekly and rates are only $6 per hour of on-line time in non-peak hours. With a printer you can then print out your own copy of the listings.

WALES

Home Interchange Ltd., 8, Hillside Farningham — Kent DA4 ODD England. Telephone: 0322 86 45 27.

INTERVAC Great Britain, 6 Siddals Lane, Allestree, Derby DE3 2DY England. Tele: 0332 55 89 31.

WEST GERMANY

Holiday Service, Ringstr. 26, D-8608, Memmelsdorf/Bamberg, West Germany. Tele: 0951 43055. DGA affiliate.

INTERVAC Germany, Verdiweg 8, 7021 Musberg, Germany. Tele: 0711 7522 69.

GOVERNMENT SERVICES AND EDUCATIONAL ORGANIZATIONS OFFERING HOME OR HOSPITALITY EXCHANGES

Academic Exchange Programs Division, Office of Academic Programs, Bureau of Educational and Cultural Affairs, U.S. Information Agency, 400 C St., S.W., Washington, DC 20547.

AFS International/Intercultural Programs, 313 E. 43rd St., New York, NY 10017. Tele: 212 949-4242. Arranges for secondary school students ages 16 to 18 to attend school in a foreign country. Students from 80 foreign countries have attended a year of high school in 3,000 United States communities, while American teenagers have attended school in 60 foreign countries.

American Host Foundation, P.O. Box 803, Garden Grove, CA 92643. Tele: 714 537-5711. Arranges for visiting teachers from the free nations of Europe to live as guests with American families, usually for two consecutive 2-week periods.

American Institute For Foreign Study, 102 Greenwich Ave., Greenwich, CT 06830. Tele: 203 869-9090. Organizes, among other things, homestays and cultural exchanges.

Association For International Practical Training, American City Bldg., Suite 217, Columbia, MD 21044. Tele: 301 997-2200. United States affiliate of the International Association for the Exchange of Students for Technical Experience, which arranges reciprocal exchanges among 48 member countries for students of engineering, architecture, agriculture, mathematics, and the sciences.

Association For World Travel Exchange, 38 W. 88th St., New York, NY 10024. Tele: 212 787-7706. Sponsors low-cost home hospitality programs for foreign students in the United States.

British American Educational Foundation, 351 E. 74th St., New York, NY 10021. Tele: 212 772-3890. Sponsors, among other things, an exchange of secondary school teachers between schools in the United States and the United Kingdom.

Council For International Exchange Of Scholars, 11 Dupont Circle, Suite 300, Washington, DC 20036. Administers, among other things, the Fulbright-Hays Act mutual educational exchange program. Maintains Register of Scholars as a resource file of U.S. citizens interested in overseas assignments.

Council On International Educational Exchange, 205 E. 42nd St., New York, NY 10017. Tele: 212 661-1414. Provides information on member institutions that promote and sponsor international education exchange. Among other things, administers study abroad programs; co-sponsors exchanges between secondary schools in the United States and schools in England, France, West Germany, Israel, Japan, Spain, and Venezuela; arranges home hospitality.

Division Of International Education, American Council on Education, 11 Dupont Circle, N.W., Rm. 300, Washington, DC 20036. Tele: 202 833-4710. Administers, among other things, the Fulbright Senior Scholar Program.

Executive Council On Foreign Diplomats, 211 E. 53rd St., New York, NY 10022. Tele: 212 688-2710. Arranges, among other things, for prominent visitors to live with local families and learn about the "real America."

Experiment In International Living, U.S. Headquarters, Kipling Rd., Brattleboro, VT 05301. Tele: 802 257-7751. Organizes, among other things, homestay living for U.S. individuals and groups when abroad and foreign visitors coming to America. Facilitates homestays for approximately 3,000 individuals and groups from nearly 100 countries in the United States each year.

Facets USA, 915 Broadway, #1705, New York, NY 10010. Tele: 212 475-4343. Created by the French Ministry of Education for the promotion and organization of student programs, including exchanges.

Faculty Exchange Center, 952 Virginia Ave., Lancaster, PA 17603. Tele: 717 393-1130. Arranges exchanges for college and university teachers as well as house exchanges for purposes of study and travel for teachers and administrators at all levels of the educational profession. Publishes a semiannual directory and house exchange supplement containing the names of the instructors and their institutions, ranks and fields of specialization, the regions where they prefer to teach, and whether they are willing to exchange homes.

Foundation For International Cooperation, 4909 Mohawk Rd., Rockford, IL 61107. Tele: 815 397-4599. Arranges, among other things, home hospitality for foreign adults and students.

Hospitality And Information Service, Meridian House, 1630 Crescent Pl., N.W., Washington, DC 20009. Tele: 202 232-3002. Arranges, among other things, informal home hospitality.

Institute of International Education, 809 United Nations Plaza, New York, NY 10017. Tele: 212 883-8200. Provides information and consultation services on all phases of educational and cultural exchange. Facilitates and administers educational exchange programs for students, scholars, artists, leaders, and specialists. Operates Register for International Service in Education data bank to match needs of foreign universities with the preferences and qualifications of U.S. scholars and post-secondary teachers.

International Center In New York, 119 W. 40th St., 11th Fl., New York, NY 10018. Tele: 212 921-8205. Assists foreign visitors with home hospitality, among other things.

International Christian Youth Exchange, U.S. Committee, 134 W. 26th St., New York, NY 10001. Tele: 212 206-7307. Operates year-long youth exchanges for 16 to 24-year-olds involving 26 countries.

International Research And Exchanges Board, 655 Third Ave., New York, NY 10017. Tele: 212 490-2002. Assists United States scholars, including humanists and social scientists, to study and conduct research in eastern Europe and the USSR and to provide opportunities for scholars from those countries to undertake similar activities in the United States.

International Student Exchange Program, Georgetown University, 1242 35th St., N.W., Washington, DC 20057. Tele: 202 625-4737. Arranges for the one-to-one exchange of United States students and foreign students between 130 colleges and universities in 26 countries.

Five hundred students were involved in 1984-85. Living quarters, whether a dormitory, apartment, bedroom, or home are exchanged between students. If students from member campuses are accepted and choose to participate, a $100 fee is required. All types of domestic student aid still apply for American students while they are out of the country.

International Visitors Information Service, 801 19th St., N.W., Washington, DC 20006. Tele: 202 872-8747. Can arrange for home hospitality on one week's notice for foreign guests.

Japan-America Student Conference, 2025 Eye St., N.W., Suite 1023, Washington, DC 20006. Tele: 202 233-4187. Offers an educational and cultural exchange program between Japanese and American university students.

National Associaton For Foreign Student Affairs, 1860 19th St., N.W., Washington, DC 20009. Facilitates and promotes, among other things, the exchange process for individuals and institutions.

National Council For International Visitors, Meridian House, 1630 Crescent Pl., N.W., Washington, DC 20009. Tele: 202 332-1028. Promotes and coordinates services at the community level which contribute to the objectives of both government and private international exchange and training programs.

National Faculty Exchange, 2101 Coliseum Blvd., E., Ft. Wayne, IN 46805. Tele: 219 482-5736. Facilitates opportunities for the exchange of faculty and administrative staff among colleges and universities in the United States. Multilateral and bilateral placement is coordinated through a pool. Service is relatively new; in 1984-85 approximately 50 faculty and staff from some of the 130 member institutions exchanged. Application form enables applicants to indicate whether they desire a home exchange as well as job exchange. Application fee is $15.

National Student Exchange, 2101 Coliseum Blvd., E., Ft. Wayne, IN 46805. Tele: 219 482-5736. Provides 1 year undergraduate exchange opportunities to approximately 2,000 students from 80 member campuses each year in the United States. Founded in 1967. Majority of students live in dormitories during exchange period; bedroom or residence exchange not normally facilitated. Application fee is $10.

Office of International Visitors, Bureau of Educational and Cultural Affairs, U.S. Information Agency, 400 C St., S.W., Washington, DC 20547. Coordinates visits of foreign dignitaries, receptions in

Washington, and the visitors' regional accommodations throughout the United States with local chapters, including hospitality or homestays.

Open Door Student Exchange, P.O. Box 1150, 124 E. Merrick Rd., Valley Stream, NY 11582. Tele: 516 825-8485. Arranges exchanges between American high schoolers and those from countries in Central America, South America, Europe, and the Middle East.

Pacific American Institute, 50 California St., Suite 200, San Francisco, CA 94111. Tele: 415 434-1206. Provides for, among other things, homestays in the United States for foreign students.

Traveling Scholar Program, c/o Committee on Institutional Cooperation, 302 E. John St., Suite 1705, Champaign, IL 61820. Tele: 217 333-8475. Enables doctoral-level graduate students from Big Ten universities and the University of Chicago to engage in short-term study or research on the campus of another participating institution.

U.S. Student Travel Service, c/o William Sloane House, 356 W. 34th St., Fl.2, New York, NY 10001. Tele: 212 947-9533. Maintains summer employment exchange programs for both American and foreign students.

Youth For Understanding, 3501 Neward St., N.W., Washington, DC 20016. Tele: 202 966-6808. Sponsors 3 teenage exchange programs that, among other things, facilitate hospitality stays for both foreign and American students.

OTHER EXCHANGE ORGANIZATIONS

Cooperative Communities of America, 2546 West Course Drive, Annapolis MD 21401. This group publishes a "Travel Guide" that lists about 150 persons offering accommodations to travelers.

Friendship Force, 575 S. Omni Intl., Atlanta, GA 30303. Tele: 404 522-9490. Arranges for groups of United States citizens to be flown to a foreign city from where an equal number of people are brought to the United States to stay in private homes.

International Center for Social Gerontology, 425 13th St., N.W., Suite 840, Washington DC 20004. One of this group's functions is to arrange group exchanges for senior citizens on low incomes.

International Cultural Exchange, Center for Arts Information, 625 Broadway, New York NY 10012. This organization publishes a small guide each March, listing 60 organizations and agencies which help facilitate international cultural exchanges.

People-to-People International, 2420 Pershing Road, Suite 300, Kansas City, MO 64108. Tele: 816 421-6343. Arranges privately among other things, home hospitality in 27 countries.

Servas (U.S. Committee), 11 John St., Room 406, New York, NY 10038. Tele: 212 267-0252. This group of approved hosts and travelers tries to promote peace through understanding and friendship through home hospitality. Members in over 90 countries. No money changes hands, and stays are usually for 2 nights. Not for people who merely want a place to stay — the friendship between host and traveler is most important.

REFERENCE SOURCES FOR EXCHANGERS

Barron's Compact Guide to Colleges, 3rd Edition, Barron's Educational Series, Inc., 113 Crossways Park Drive, Woodbury, NY 11797. A list of over 350 U.S. schools, with addresses and telephone numbers.

The World of Learning. This large book lists schools in over 140 countries with their addresses, size of faculty, and student enrollment.

Where to Phone NCIV Across the U.S.A., National Council for International Visitors, Meridian House, 1630 Crescent Place N.W., Washington, DC 20009. This free brochure gives names and telephone numbers of NCIV community organizations that have signified a willingness to assist unsponsored visitors from abroad who are traveling on their own.

IMS Ayer Directory. This book, found in most library reference rooms, lists U.S. and Canadian newspapers not found in this book's United States Country Appendix.

National Faculty Directory, Gale Research Company, Book Tower, Detroit, MI 48226. This reference work categorizes 525, 000 faculty members at over 3,400 U.S. and Canadian junior colleges, colleges, and universities. Valuable if you want to personalize letters going to school department teachers.

Foreign Area Program at North American Universities: A Directory, California Institute of Public Affairs, P.O. Box 10, Claremont, CA 91711. Gives descriptions of study abroad programs offered by U.S. schools.

National Directory of Community Organizations Serving Short-Term International Visitors, National Council for International Visitors, Meridian House, 1630 Crescent Place, N.W., Washington, DC 20009. This lists about 150 groups which provide services for international visitors. Addresses included.

International Handbook of Universities and Other Institutions of Higher Education, International Association of Universities, 1 rue Miollis, F-75732 Paris Cedex 15, France. Found in most libraries, this guide gives you the addresses of schools not listed in this book's appendix B.

American Universities and Colleges, American Council on Education, One Dupont Circle, N.W., Washington, DC 20036. This standard reference book lists over 1,700 4-year universities in the U.S.

Education Directory: Colleges and Universities, National Center for Educational Statistics, Education Department, 400 Maryland Avenue, S.W., Washington, DC 20202. Lists 3,100 colleges in the U.S., with addresses and telephone numbers.

Foreign Embassies in the United States, International Division, Chamber of Commerce of the United States, 1615 H Street, N.W., Washington, DC 20062. The brochure "Employment Abroad: Facts and Fallacies," lists all embassies in the U.S. which have information on employment for aliens.

Whole World Handbook, Council on International Educational Exchange. This is a good, inexpensive guide for students about studying, working, and traveling abroad.

Host Family Survival Kit: A Guide For American Host Families, by Nancy King and Ken Huff, Intercultural Press, Inc., P.O. Box 76B, Yarmouth, Maine 04096. Smart tips if your son or daughter is exchanging bedrooms with a foreign student. $8.95.

Two Years In The Melting Pot, by Liu Zongren, Intercultural Press, Inc., P.O. Box 76B, Yarmouth, Maine 04096. An insightful account by Chinese journalist Zongren of American culture while the author was an exchange scholar in Chicago for 2 years. Many of Zongren's observations and points are applicable to anyone going to any other radically different from his or her own. $8.95.

NAFSA Directory, National Association for Foreign Student Affairs, 1860 19th St., NW, Washington, DC 20009. A valuable and comprehensive guide for those interested in making an educational exchange or for those interested in exchanging with teachers, scholars or students. Includes contact names of people at organizations and colleges who facilitate exchanges. $25.00 for non-members.

TRANSLATION SERVICES

Conway Associates International Inc., 109 East 42nd Street, New York, NY 10017. Minimum charge for translating a classified ad is approximately $30.

ICCS-LanFranco Corp., 1-15-9 Tabata-kita-ku, Tokyo 114, Japan.

LanFranco Corp., One Hallidie Plaza, Suite 803, San Francisco, CA 94102. Tele: 415 434-2700. Minimum charge for translating a classified ad is approximately $45 for all LanFranco offices.

LanFranco Corp., Mid-Eastern Language Service, 24 E. 21st Street, 6th Floor, New York, NY 10010. Tele: 212 505-0488.

LanFranco Corp., 1052 W. 6th Street, Suite 602, Los Angeles, CA 90017. Tele: 213 481-8088.

APPENDIX B

COUNTRIES

This Appendix lists colleges and universities, major newspapers and community host organizations by country; in short, the most likely alternative sources for you to find home exchange partners.

The educational institutions listed will enable you to send packets of notices to departmental secretaries and classified advertisements to student body newspapers, while you can telephone or write the major newspapers to place classified ads. Unless specified, the newspapers listed here are in the primary language of the country in question. Placing an ad in a newspaper that prints the native language of a country will usually mean broader exposure for your offer, as well as a different readership, one that is more representative of the population. English language newspapers in Japan or South Korea, for example, are primarily read by affluent foreign businessmen, and not primarily by Japanese or Koreans.

If the information you need, whether a newspaper, community host organization, or university address, is not listed here, look in appendix A for source books and guides that are more inclusive.

COLLEGES AND UNIVERSITIES

ALGERIA

Alger: The University of Alger.
Annaba: The University of Annaba.
Constantine: The University of Constantine.
Oran: The University of Oran.

AUSTRALIA

New South Wales

Macquarie University, North Ryde, New South Wales, 2113.
University of New South Wales, P.O. Box 1, Kensington, NSW 2033.
The University of Sydney, Sydney, New South Wales, 2006.
The University of Wollongong, P.O. Box 1144, Wollongong, NSW 2500.

Queensland

Griffith University, Nathan, Queensland 4111.
The University of Queensland, St. Lucia, Queensland, 4067.
Queensland Institute of Technology, George Street, Brisbane, Queensland, 4000.

South Australia

The Flinders University of South Australia, Bedford Park, South Australia, 5042.
The University of Adelaide, Adelaide, South Australia, 5000.

Western Australia

Murdoch University, Murdoch, Western Australia, 6153.
The University of Western Australia, Nedlands, Western Australia, 6009.

Victoria

La Trobe University, Bundoora, Victoria, 3083.
Deakin University, Victoria, 3217.
University of Melbourne, Parkville, Victoria 3052.
Royal Melbourne Institute of Technology, Box 2476V, GPO Melbourne, Victoria, 3001.

BAHAMAS
The College of The Bahamas, P.O. Box N 4912, Nassau.

BARBADOS
St. John

Codrington College (Theology), St. John, Barbados, West Indies.

St. Michael

University of the West Indies, Cave Hill, St. Michael, Barbados, West Indies.
Samuel Jackman Prescod Polytechnic, Belmont Road, St. Michael, Barbados, West Indies.
Academy of Commerce and Technical Studies, Chepstow River Road, St. Michael, Barbados, West Indies.
Macon Business Academy, Emtage Electric Building, River Road, St. Michael, Barbados, West Indies.

St. Phillip

Baptist Theological College, Fortescue Plantation, St. Phillip, Barbados, West Indies.

BELGIUM
Universite Libre De Bruxelles, 50, avenue Franklin D. Roosevelt, 1050 Bruxelles.
Universite De L'Etat A Liege, 7, place du 20 aout, 4000 Liege.
Rijksuniversiteit Te Gent, Sint-Pietersnieuwstraat 25, 9000 Gent.

BOLIVIA
Cochabamba: Universidad Mayor de San Simon, Calle Oquendo-Sucre, Cochabamba. Tele: 25501.
La Paz: Universidad Mayor de San Andres, Avda. Villazon No. 1995, La Paz. Tele: 362041.
Oruro: Universidad Tecnica de Oruro, Avda. 6 de Octubre No. 1209, Oruro. Tele: 50106.
Potosi: Universidad Mayor Tomas Frias, Casilla No. 36, Potosi. Tele: 3020.
Santa Cruz: Universidad Mayor Gabriel Rene Moreno, Plaza 14 de Septiembre, Casilla No. 702, Santa Cruz. Tele: 23780.

Sucre: Universidad Mayor Real y Pontificia, "San Francisco Xavier," Casilla No. 212, Suce. Tele: 3245.
Tarija: Universidad Mayor Juan Misael Saracho, Casilla No. 51, Tarija. Tele: 3110.
Trinidad: Universidad Mayor Gral. Jose Ballivian, Casilla No. 38, Trinidad, Beni. Tele: 558.

BRAZIL

Universidade Federal Do Rio De Janeiro, Avenida Brigadeiro Trompowsky, s/n, 20.000 Rio De Janeiro RJ.
Pontificia Universidade Catolica Do Rio De Janeiro, Rua Marques De Sao Vicente, 225, 20.000 Rio De Janeiro RJ.
Universidade De Sao Paulo, Cidade Universitaria Armando S. De Oliveira, 05508 Sao Paulo SP.
Universidade Federal Do Parana, Avenida XV De Novembro, 1299, Curitiba Parana.

CANADA

The University of Alberta, Edmonton, Alberta T6G 2M7.
The University of British Columbia, 2075 Wesbrook Mall, Vancouver, British Columbia V6T 1W5.
The University of Calgary, 2920 24th Avenue North West, Calgary, Alberta T2N 1N4.
McGill University, Montreal, Quebec H3A 2T5.
University of Toronto, Toronto, Ontario M5S 1A1.

COSTA RICA

Cartago

Instituto Tecnologico de Costa Rica, Apartado 159, Cartago.

Escazu

Universidad de la Paz, Escazu.

Heredia

Universidad Nacional, Apartado 86, Heredia.

San Jose

Universidad de Costa Rica, San Pedro Montes de Oca.
Universidad Autonoma de Centro America, Apartado 7637, San Jose.
Universidad Estatal a Distancia, Apartado 2 1001 MOPT, San Jose.

CYPRUS
The Higher College of Technology, P.O. Box 4729, Palouriotissa, Nicosia. Tele: 31355.
College of Arts and Science, P.O. Box 2140, Nicosia. Tele: 41125.
English Tutorial Centre, P.O. Box 4621, Nicosia. Tele: 41603.

CZECHOSLOVAKIA
Univerzita Karlova v Praze, Ovocny trh 5, 116 36, Praha 1. Tele: 022 84419.
Univerzita Komenskeho v Bratislave, Safarikovo nam. 6, 885 45 Bratislava. Tele: 0580 415.
Univerzita Jana Evangelisty Purkyne v Brne, Arne Novaka 1, 601 77 Brno. Tele: 0597 11.
Univerzita Palacheho v Olomouci, Krizkovskeho 10, 771 47 Olomouc. Tele: 0224 41.

DENMARK
Aarhus Universitet (University of Aarhus), Ndr. Ringgade 1, 8000 Aarhus C.
Kobenhavns Universitet (University of Copenhagen), Frue Plads, 1168 Kobenhavn K.

EGYPT
Alexandria
Alexandria University, 3 El-Gueish Avenue, Shatby, Alexandria.

Cairo
Cairo University, El-Orman, Cairo.
Ain-Shams University, El-Abbasia, Cairo.
Al-Azhar University, El-Darrasa, Cairo.

ENGLAND
University of Birmingham, P.O. Box 363, Edgbaston, Birmingham B15 2TT.
University of Bradford, Bradford, West Yorkshire BD7 1DP.
Brunel University, Uxbridge, Middlesex UB8 3PH.

University College at Buckingham, Buckingham MK18 1EG.
University of Cambridge, University Registry, The Old Schools, Cambridge CB2 1TN.
University of Essex, Wivenhoe Park, Colchester CO4 3SQ.
University of Keele, Keele, Staffordshire ST5 5BG.
University of Kent at Canterbury, Kent CT2 7NZ.
University of Leeds, Leeds LS2 9JT.
University of Liverpool, P.O. Box 147, Liverpool L69 3BX.
University of London, Senate House, London WC1E 7HU.
University of Manchester, Oxford Road, Manchester M13 9PL.
University of Nottingham, University Park, Nottingham NG7 2RD.
University of Sheffield, Sheffield S10 2TN.
University of Surrey, Guildford, Surrey GU2 5XH.

FINLAND

Helsingin Yliopisto (University of Helsinki), Hallituskatu 8, 00100 Helsinki 10.

FRANCE

Universite De Provence (Aix-Marseille I), 3, place Victor-Hugo, 13331 Marseille Cedex 3.
Universite De Bordeaux I, 351, cours de la Liberation, 33405 Talence Cedex.
Universite Pantheon-Sorbonne (Paris I), 12, place du Pantheon, 75231 Paris Cedex 05.
Universite De Paris — SUD (Paris XI), 11, rue Georges Clemenceau 91405 Orsay Cedex.
Universite De Rennes (Rennes I), 2, rue du Thabor, 35000 Rennes.
Universite Louis-Pasteur (Strasbourge I), 4, rue Blaise Pascal, B.P. 1032/F 67070 Strasbourg Cedex.
Universite De Toulouse — Le Mirail (Toulouse II), 109 bis, rue Vauquelin 31081 Toulouse Cedex.

GREECE

University of Athens, Athens.
University of Thessaloniki, Thessaloniki.
University of Patra, Patra.

GUATEMALA

Universidad de San Carlos de Guatemala, Ciudad Universitaria, zona 12, Guatemala, Guatemala. Tele: 76 07 90/94, or 76 09 85/88.
Universidad Rafael Landivar, Campus Vista Hermosa III, zona 16, Guatemala, Guatemala. Tele: 69 21 51, or 69 26 21.
Universidad Dr. Mariano Galvez, 3a. avenida 9-00, zona 2, Interior El Zapote, Guatemala, Guatemala. Tele: 27 4 86, or 53 42 71.
Universidad del Valle, 11 calle 15-79, zona 15, Vista Hermosa III, Guatemala, Guatemala. Tele: 69 25 63, or 69 27 76.

GUYANA

The University of Guyana, Turkeyen, Greater Georgetown.
Queen's College, Camp Road, Georgetown.

ICELAND

Akureyri

Akureyri Higher Secondary Grammar School, Menntastolinn a Akureyri, 600 Akureyri.

Reykjavik

University of Iceland, Sudurgata, 101 Reykjavik.
The Reykjavik Higher Secondary Grammer School, Menntaskolinn i Reykjavik, Laekjargata, 101 Reykjavik.
The Commercial College of Iceland, Verslunarskili Islands, Grundarstig 24, 101 Reykjavik.

INDIA

Bombay: University of Bombay, M.G. Road, Fort, Bombay 400032 (Maharashtra). Tele: 273623.
Calcutta: University of Calcutta, 87/1 College Street, Calcutta 700073 (West Bengal). Tele: 343014.
Delhi: University of Delhi, Delhi 110007. Tele: 221421.
Madras: University of Madras, University Buildings, Madras 600005 (Tamil Nadu). Tele: 848778.

INDONESIA

University of Indonesia, Jalan Salemba Raya 4, Jakarta Pusat. Tele: 882992 or 882955.
Bandung Institute of Technology, Jalan Tamansari 64, Bandung, Jawa Barat. Tele: 83047 or 83048.

Bogor Institute of Agriculture, Jalan Raya Pajajaran, Jawa Barat. Tele: 23081 or 233082.
Gajah Mada University, Bulaksumur, Yogyakarta, Jawa Tengah. Tele: 88688.

IRELAND
Trinity College, College Green, Dublin 2.
University College Dublin, Belfield, Dublin 4.
University College Cork, Cork.
University College Galway, Galway.

ISRAEL
Hebrew University, Usuat Scopus, Jerusalem.
Tel Aviv University, Ramat Aviv.
Ben Gurion University, Beer Sheva.

ITALY
Universita Statali:

Bari(70100) Palazzo Ateneo.
Padova (35100), v. 8 Febbraio 2.
Palermo (90133), v. Maqueda 172.
Roma (00100), ple delle Scienze.
Trieste (23127),

JAPAN
Nihon University, 2-6-16, Nishi-Kanda, Chiyoda-ku, Tokyo 101.
Waseda University, 1-6-1, Nishi-Waseda, Shinjuku-ku, Tokyo 160.
Tokai University 2-28-4, Tomigaya, Shibuya-ku, Tokyo 151.
Meiji University, 1-1, Kanda-Surugadai, Chiyoda-Ku, Tokyo 101.

JORDAN
Amman

University of Jordan, Jubeiha, Amman.
Yarmouk University, P.O. Box 20184, Amman.

Mu'tah

Mu'tah University, Mu'tan.

KUWAIT
Kuwait University, Kuwait City. Largest facilities are those of Arts, Science, Commerce, and Education.

MALAYSIA

Kuala Lumpur

University of Malaysia, Lembah Pantai, Kuala Lumpur.
Universiti Teknologi Malaysia, Jalan Gurney, Kuala Lumpur.

Selangor

National University, Bangi, Selangor.
University of Agriculture, Serbang, Selangor.

MEXICO

Universidad Autonoma Metropolitana, Avila Camacho 90, 10, D.F.
Universidad Nacional Autonoma De Mexico, Ciudad Universitaria, Villa Obregon, 20, D.F.
Universidad Autonoma De Nuevo Leon, Ciudad Universitaria, San Nicolas de los Garza.
Universidad De Guadalajara, Avenida Juarez No. 975, Guadalajara.

MOROCCO

Casablanca

Hassan II University, Casablanca. Major faculties are in law, medicine, and pharmacy.
Mohammedia School of Engineering, Casablanca.

Fes

Quaraouiyine University, Fes. Major faculties include law and theology.

Rabat

Mahammed V University, Rabat. Major faculties include law, arts and letters, medicine, and pharmacy.

NETHERLANDS

Universiteit van Amsterdam, Dienst Studentenwelzijnszorg, Nieuwe Doelenstraat 9, 1012 CP Amsterdam.
Erasmus-Universiteit Rotterdam, Bureau Buitenlandse Betrekkingen, Postbus 1738, 3000 DR Rotterdam.
Rijksuniversiteit Utrecht, Bureau College van Dekanen, Postbus 202, 3500 AE Utrecht.

NORWAY
Universitetet I Bergen, Museplass 1, 5014 Bergen.
Universitetet I Oslo, Box 1076, Blindern, Oslo 3.

PAKISTAN
Islamabad: Quaide-e-Azam University, Islamabad.
Karachi: University of Karachi, Karachi.
Lahore: University of Punjab, Lahore.
Peshawar: Peshawar University, Peshawar.

PANAMA
Universidad de Panama, Estafeta Universitaria, Panama, Republica de Panama.
Universidad Santa Maria La Antigua, Apartado 6-1696, 6A-Dorado, Panama, Republica de Panama.
Universidad Tecnologica de Panama, Apartodo 6-2894, 6A-Dorado, Panama, Republica de Panama.

PERU
Universidad Nacional Mayor De San Marcos (National University of San Marcos), Avenida Republica de Chile 295, Apartado 454, Lima. Oldest University in the Americas, specializing in medicine, letters, pharmacy, biochemistry.
Universidad Del Pacifico (University of the Pacific), Avenida Salaverry 2020, Lince, Apartado 4683. Economics, business administration.
Universidad Nacional Agraria (National Agrarian University), La Molina s/n, Apartado 456, Lima. Agriculture, forestry.
Universidad Nacional Federico Villarreal (National University "Federico Villarreal"), Avenida Nicolas de Pierola 262, Apartado 1518, Lima 1. Administrative sciences, architecture, education.

PHILIPPINES
Manila
Far Eastern University, Claro M. Recto Ave., Manila.
University of the East, Morayta Ave., Manila.
University of Santo Tomas, Espana Ext. Blvd., Sampaloc, Manila.

Quezon City
University of the Philippines, Diliman, Quezon City.

PORTUGAL
Universidade De Coimbra, Coimbra.
Universidade Classica De Lisboa (University of Lisbon), Alameda da Universitario, 1966 Lisboa Codex.
Universidade Do Porto, Rua D. Manuel II, 4003 Porto Codex.

PUERTO RICO
The University of Puerto Rico/Rio Piedras, Rio Piedras 00931.

SAUDI ARABIA
Dhahran
University of Petroleum and Minerals, Dhahran International Airport, P.O. Box 144, Dhahran. Tele: 894 2911 or 860 2000.

Eastern Province
King Faisal University, Eastern Province, P.O. Box 1982. Tele: 832 6443 or 832 2726.

Jeddah
King Abdulaziz University, P.O. Box 1540, Mecca Road, Jeddah. Tele: 687 9033 or 689 9130.

Mecca
Institute of Education, Mecca.
Umm Al-Qura University, P.O. Box 715, Mecca. Tele: 556 5321.

Medina
Islamic University, P.O. Box 170, Medina. Tele: 822-4080 or 822 4402.

Riyadh
College of Arabic Language, Riyadh.
King Saud University, Riyadh. Tele: 476 7296.

SCOTLAND
University of Aberdeen, Aberdeen AB9 1FX.
University of Edinburgh, Old College, South Bridge, Edinburgh EH8 9YL.
University of Glasgow, Glasgow G12 8QQ.

SOUTH AFRICA
University of Pretoria, Brooklyn, Pretoria 0181.
University of Stellenbosch, Stellenbosch 7600.
University of the Witwaterstrand, 1, Jan Smuts Ave., Johannesburg 2001.
University of Natal, King George V Ave., Durban 4001.

SOUTH KOREA

Korea University, 1-2, 5-ga, Anam-dong, Songbuk-gu, Seoul.
Hanyang University, 17, Haengdang-dong, Songdong-gu, Seoul.
Seoul National University, San 56-1, Sinrim-dong, Kwanak-gu, Seoul.
Yonsei University, 134, Sinchon-dong, Sodaemun-gu, Seoul.

SPAIN

Universidad Autonoma De Barcelona, Campus Universitario de Bellaterra, Cerdanyola, Barcelona 2.
Universidad De Granada, Plaza de la Universidad, Granada.
Universidad Complutense De Madrid (University of Madrid), Pabellon de Gobierno, Ciudad Universitaria, Madrid 3.
Universidad De Valencia, Nave 2, Valencia 3.

SWEDEN

Goteborgs Universitet, Vasaparken, 41124 Goteborg.
Lunds Universitet, Fack, 221-01 Lund.
Stockholms Universitet, 106 91 Stockholm.
Uppsala Universitet, P.O. Box 256, 751 05 Uppsala.

SWITZERLAND

University of Geneva, Place de l'Universite 3, CH-1211 Geneva 4.
University of Zurich, Ramistrasse 71, CH-8006 Aurich.
St. Gall College of Economics and Social Science, Dufourstrasse 50, CH-9000 St. Gallen.

TRINIDAD AND TOBAGO

University of the West Indies, St. Augustine Campus, St. Augustine, Trinidad, Trinidad and Tobago. Tele: 809 662-7171.
Corinth Teachers College, C-O Cocoyea P O, Port of Spain, Trinidad, Trinidad and Tobago. Tele: 809 652-4445.
Naparima Teachers College, Paradise Hill, Port of Spain, Trinidad, Trinidad and Tobago. Tele: 809 652-3210.
The Valsayn Teachers College, Caroni Gravel Road, Port of Spain, Trinidad, Trinidad and Tobago. Tele: 809 662-2417.

TURKEY

Ankara
Ankara Universitesi, Ankara.
Hacettepe Universitesi, Ankara.

Bogazici Universitesi, Istanbul.
Istanbul Universitesi, Istanbul.

UGANDA

Gulu

Sir Samuel Baker College, P.O. Box 100, Gulu.

Kampala

Kings College, Budo, P.O. Box 7121, Kampala.
Makerere University, P.O. Box 7062, Kampala.

Mbale

Nabumali High School, P.O. Box 902, Mbale.

Mbarara

Ntare School, P.O. Box 57, Mbarara.

UNITED STATES

Alabama

University of Alabama, University AL 35486.
Auburn University, Auburn AL 36830.

Arizona

Arizona State University, Tempe AZ 85281.
University of Arizona, Tucson AZ 85721.

Arkansas

University of Arkansas, Fayetteville AR 72701.

California

California State University, Fullerton, Fullerton CA 92634.
California State University, Hayward, Hayward CA 94542.
California State University, Long Beach, 1250 Bellflower Blvd., Long Beach CA 90840.
California State University, Los Angeles, 5151 State University Drive, Los Angeles CA 90032.
California State University, Sacramento, 6000 J Street, Sacramento CA 95819.
Humboldt State University, Arcata CA 95521.
San Diego State University, 5300 Campanile Drive, San Diego CA 92182.
San Jose State University, Washington Square, San Jose CA 95192.
University of California at Berkeley, Berkley CA 94720.
University of California at Los Angeles, Los Angeles CA 90024.
University of California at Santa Barbara, Santa Barbara CA 93106.
University of Southern California, Los Angeles CA 90007.
Stanford University, Stanford CA 94035.

Colorado

Colorado State University, Fort Collins CO 80523.
University of Colorado at Boulder, Boulder CO 80302.

Connecticut

University of Connecticut, Storrs CT 06268.
Yale University, New Haven CT 06520.

Delaware

University of Delaware, Newark DE 19711.

District Of Columbia

Georgetown University, Washington DC 20057.
George Washington University, Washington DC 20052.

Florida

Florida State University, Tallahassee FL 32306.
University of Florida, Gainesville FL 32611.
University of Miami, Coral Gables FL 33124.

Georgia

University of Georgia, Athens GA 30605.
Georgia State University, Atlanta GA 30303.

Idaho

Idaho State University, Pocatello, Idaho 23209.

Illinois

De Paul University, Chicago IL 60604.
University of Illinois at Champaign-Urbana, Urbana IL 61801.
Loyola University of Chicago, Chicago IL 60611
Southern Illinois University at Carbondale, Carbondale IL 62901.

Indiana

Indiana University, Bloomington IN 47401.
University of Notre Dame, Notre Dame IN 46556.
Purdue University, West Lafayette IN 47907.

Iowa

Iowa State University, Ames IA 50011.
University of Iowa, Iowa City IA 52242.

Kansas

Kansas State University, Manhattan KS 66506.
University of Kansas, Lawrence KA 66045.
Wichita State University, Wichita KS 67208.

Kentucky
University of Kentucky, Lexington KY 40506.
University of Louisville, Louisville KY 40208.

Louisiana
Louisiana State University at Baton Rouge, Baton Rouge LA 70803.

Maryland
University of Maryland at College Park, College Park MD 20742.

Massachusetts
Boston University, Boston MA 02215.
Harvard University (with Radcliffe College), Cambridge MA 02138.
Massachusetts Institute of Technology, Cambridge MA 02139.
University of Massachusetts at Amherst, Amherst MA 01002.
Northeastern University, Boston MA 02115.

Michigan
Michigan State University, East Lansing MI 48824.
University of Michigan, Ann Arbor MI 48104.
Wayne State University, Detroit MI 48202.

Minnesota
University of Minnesota, Minneapolis MN 55455.

Missouri
University of Missouri at Columbia, Columbia MO 65201.
St. Louis University, St. Louis MO 63103.

Nebraska
University of Nebraska at Lincoln, Lincoln NE 68508.

New Jersey
Rutgers College of Rutgers University, New Brunswick NJ 08903.

New Mexico
University of New Mexico, Albuquerque NM 87131.

New York
Columbia College of Columbia University, New York NY 10027.
Cornell University, Ithaca NY 14853.
Hunter College/City University of New York, New York NY 10021.
State University of New York at Buffalo, Buffalo NY 14214.
New York University, New York NY 10003.
Rochester Institute of Technology, Rochester NY 14623.
Syracuse University, Syracuse NY 13210.

North Carolina

University of North Carolina at Chapel Hill, Chapel Hill 27514.

Ohio

Bowling Green State University, Bowling Green OH 43403.
University of Cincinnati, Cincinnati OH 45221.
Kent State University, Kent OH 44242.
Ohio State University, Columbus OH 43210.

Oklahoma

Oklahoma State University, Stillwater OK 74074.
University of Oklahoma, Norman OK 73019.

Oregon

Oregon State University, Corvallis OR 97331.
University of Oregon, Eugene OR 97403.

Pennsylvania

Pennsylvania State University, University Park PA 16802.
University of Pennsylvania, Philadelphia PA 19104.
University of Pittsburgh, Pittsburgh PA 15213.
Temple University, Philadelphia PA 19122.

South Carolina

University of South Carolina, Columbia SC 29208.

Texas

University of Houston/Central Campus, Houston TX 77004.
Texas A & M University, College Station TX 77843.
Texas Tech University, Lubbock TX 79409.
University of Texas at Austin, Austin TX 78712.

Utah

Brigham Young University, Provo UT 84602.
University of Utah, Salt Lake City UT 84112.

Virginia

The University of Virginia, Charlottesville VA 22903.

Washington

University of Washington, Seattle WA 98105.

Wisconsin

Marquette University, Milwaukee WI 53233.

WALES

University College of Wales, Aberystwyth, Dyfed SY23 2AX.
University College of North Wales, Bangor, Gwynedd LL57 2DG.
University College, Cardiff, P.O. Box 78, Cardiff CF1 1XL.

WEST GERMANY

Colleges and Universities

Bonn: Rheinische Friedrich-Wilhelms-Universitat, Akademisches Auslandsamt, NassestraBe 15, 5300 Bonn.
Bremen: Universitat Akademische Auslandsangelegenheiten, Postfach 33 04 40, 2800 Bremen 33.
Dortmund: Universitat, Akademisches Auslandsamt, Hauptbauflache, Gebaude 1, Chemietechnik, 4600 Dortmund-Eichlinghofen.
Dusseldorf: Universitat, Akademisches Auslandsamt, UniversitatsstraBe 1, 4000 Dusseldorf.
Frankfurt: Johann-Wolfgang-Goethe-Universitat, Akademisches Auslandsamt, Senckenberganlage 31, Postfach 11 19 32, 6000 Frankfurt/Main.
Hamburg: Universitat, Akademisches Auslandsamt, Edmund-Siemers-Allee 1, 2000 Hamburg 13.
Hannover: Medizinische Hochschule, Akademische Abteilung/Auslandsamt, Karl-Wiechert-Allee 9, 3000 Hannover 61.

YUGOSLAVIA

Belgrade: University of Belgrade, Studentski trg 1, 11000 Beograd.
Novi Sad: University of Novi Sad, Veljka Vlanhovica 3, 21000 Novi Sad.
Pristina: University of Kosovo, Marsala Tita bb, 38000 Pristina.
Sarajevo: University of Sarajevo, Obala 7, 71000, Sarajevo.
Skopje: "Kiril and Metodij" University, Bulevar Goce Delceva bb, 91000 Skopje.
Titograd: "Veljko Vlahovic" University, Ljesko polje bb, 81000 Titograd.
Zagreb: University of Zagreb, Trg Marsala Tita 14, 41000 Zagreb.

MAJOR NEWSPAPERS

ALGERIA

El Moudjahid, Algeria.
El Nasr, Algeria.
Both of these papers publish French and Arabic editions. Letters written in English might be understood.

AUSTRALIA

South Australia
Adelaide: **The Advertiser**, Advertiser Newspapers Ltd., 121 King William St., GPO Box 339, Adelaide 5001.

Queensland
Brisbane: **The Courier Mail**, Queensland Newspapers Pty. Ltd., GPO Box 130, Campbell St., Bowen Hills, Brisbane 4001.

New South Wales
Sydney: **Australian Financial Review** (national business newspaper), John Fairfax & Sons Ltd., GPO Box 506, Sydney 2001.
Sydney: **Daily Mirror**, Mirror Newspapers Ltd., 2 Holt St., Sydney 2010.

Western Australia
Perth: **The West Australian**, West Australian Newspapers Ltd., P.O. Box D162, 125 St. George's Tce., Perth 6001.

Victoria
Melbourne: **The Herald**, The Herald & Weekly Times Ltd., 44-74 Flinders St., Melbourne 3000.

AUSTRIA

Die Presse (business newspaper), Muthgasse 2A, 1191 Vienna.
Kurier, 1072, Lindengasse 52, A-1072 Vienna.
Neue Kronen-Zeitung, Muthgasse 2, 1190 Vienna.

BAHAMAS

The Nassau Guardian, P.O. Box N 3011, Nassau.
The Tribune, P.O. Box N 3207, Nassau.
Official language is English.

BARBADOS

The Advocate-News Company Ltd., Fontabelle, St. Michael, Barbados, West Indies.
The Nation Publishing Company Ltd., Fontabelle, St. Michael, Barbados, West Indies.

BELGIUM

Antwerpen: Gazet Van Antwerpen/Gazet Van Mechelen, Katwilgweg 2, B-2050 Antwerp.
Brussels: Het Laatste Nieuws, 105-107 Boulevard Em., Jacqmain, 1000 Brussels.
Ghent: Het Volk, Forelstraat, 22, 9000 Ghent.
Liege: La Meuse, 8/10 Blvd., de la Sauveniere, 4000 Liege.

BOLIVIA

Cochabamba: Los Tiempos, Santivanez 4110, Cochabamba. Tele: 28286 or 28228.

La Paz: El Diario, calle Loayza 118, La Paz. Tele: 322172 or 372340.
Presincia, Casilla 1451, La Paz. Tele: 322172 or 372340.

Oruro: La Patria, Calle Camacho 1892, Oruro. Tele: 50780.

Santa Cruz: El Mundo, Casilla 1984, Santa Cruz.

The dominant language is Spanish. Letters written in English will be understood.

BRAZIL

Rio De Janeiro:

Jornal Do Brasil, Avenida Brasil, 500, Rio De Janeiro RJ CEP 20.000.
O Globo, Rua Irineu Marinho, 35, 20.000 Rio De Janeiro RJ.

Sao Paulo

O Estado De Sao Paulo, Avenida Engenheiro Caetano Alvares, 55, 02550 Sao Paulo SP.
Folha da Tarde, Alameda Barao De Limeira, 425, 01202 Sao Paulo SP.
Address your envelope to the classified ad department as follows: "Seqao de Anuncios Classificados." Portuguese is the main language. Letters in English will be understood.

CANADA

Alberta

Calgary: The Calgary Herald, Southam Inc., 215 16 St. SE, Calgary, AB T2P OW8.
Edmonton: Edmonton Journal, 10006 101 St., Edmonton, AB T5J 2S6.

British Columbia

Vancouver: The Vancouver Sun, 2250 Granville St., Vancouver, British Columbia V6H 3G2.
Victoria: Times-Colonist, 2621 Douglas St., Victoria, British Columbia V8W 2N4.

Ontario

Ottawa: The Citizen, 1101 Baxter Road, P.O. Box 5020, Ottawa, Ontario K2C 3M4.
Toronto: The Toronto Star, One Yonge St., Toronto, Ontario M5E 1E6.

Quebec

Montreal: Le Journal de Montreal (French), 155 Port Royal W., Montreal, PQ H3L 2B1.

COSTA RICA

La Gaceta, Imprenta Nacional, San Jose.
La Nacion, Apartado Postal 10138, San Jose.
La Prensa Libre, Apartado Postal 1533, San Jose.
La Republica, Apartado Postal 2130, San Jose.

The Tico Times (English), Apartado Postal 4632, San Jose.
Universidad , Apartado Postal 21, Ciudad Universitaria "Rodrigo Facio," San Pedro de Montes de Oca, San Jose.
Official language is Spanish but English is widely understood.

CYPRUS

Nicosia: **Phileleftheros**, 12 Them. Dervi St. & 33 Vas. Frederikis St., "Palai De Ivouar" Bldg., P.O. Box 1094. Tele: 463922.
Nicosia: **Cyprus Mail** (English), 24 Vas. Voulgaroctonos St. Tele: 462074-5.
Nicosia: **Ergatimo Vima**, 11-35 Archermou St. Tele:473192-7.
Strovolos: **Apogevmatini**, 5 Aegaleo St. Tele: 443858.
Dominant language is Greek but many can understand English.

CZECHOSLOVAKIA

Rude Pravo, Sefredaktor Zdenek Horeni, Na Porici 30, 11286 Praha 1. Tele: 024 9851.

DENMARK

Copenhagen: **Ekstra Bladet**, Raadhuspladsen 37, 1585 Copenhagen V.
Esbjerg: **Vestkysten**, Banegardspladsen, 6700 Esberg.
Hillerod: **Frederiksborg Amts Avis**, Milnersvej 44, 3400 Hillerod.
Odense: **Fyens Stiftstidende Morgenposten**, Jernbanegade 1, 5100 Odense C.

EGYPT

Al Ahram, Galla St., Cairo. Tele: 0755 500.
Al Akhbar, 3 Sahafa St., Cairo. Tele: 0758 888.
Egyptian Gazette (English), 24 Zakaria Ahmed, Cairo. Tele: 0741 611, or 0751 511.
El Gomhoria, 241 Zakaria Ahmed St., Cairo. Tele: 0744 166.
Letters written in English will be understood by newspaper staffs.

ENGLAND

Birmingham

Birmingham Evening Mail, 28 Colmore Circus, Queensway, Birmingham.

Coventry

Coventry Evening Telegraph, Coorporation St., Conventry, West Midlands.

Derby
Derby Evening Telegraph, Albert St., Derby.

Hull
The Daily Mail, 84-86 Jameson St., Hull, Humberside.

Leeds
Evening Post, Wellington St., Leeds, West Yorks.

Leicester
Leicester Mercury, St. George St., Leicester.

Liverpool
Liverpool Echo, Old Hall St., Liverpool.

London
Daily Express, 121-128 Fleet St., London EC4.
Financial Times (business newspaper), 10 Cannon St., London EC4.
Times, New Printing House Sq., Gray's Inn Rd., London WC1.

Manchester
Manchester Ev'ng News, 164 Deansgate, Manchester.

Newcastle-Upon-Tyne
Evening Chronicle, Groat Market, Newcastle-Upon-Tyne.

Nottingham
Nottingham Evening Post, Forman St., Nottingham.

Oldham
Evening Chronicle, Union St., Oldham, Lancs.

Sheffield
The Star, York St., Sheffield, South Yorks.

Stoke-On-Trent
Evening Sentinel, Foundry St., Hanley, Stoke-On-Trent, Staffs.

Wolverhampton
Express & Star, 50-53 Queen St., Wolverhampton, West Midlands.

FINLAND

Helsinki: Hilsingin Sanomat, Ludviginkatu 1, Box 240, 00101 Helsinki 10.
Jyvaskyla: Keskisuomalainen, Box 159, Aholaidantie 3, 40101, Jyvaskyla 10.
Oulu: Kaleva, Postilokero 70, 90101, Oulu 10.
Pori: Satakunnan Kansa, Box 58, 28101, Pori 10.

FRANCE

Rennes

Oueste-France, BP 586, 35012 Rennes Cedex.

Lille

La Voix Du Nord, 8, Place du General de Gaulle, 59000 Lille.

Paris

France-Sior, 100, rue Reaumur, 75060 Paris Cedex 02.
Le Monde, 5, rue des Italiens, 75427 Paris Cedex 09.
Address your envelope to the classified ad department as follows: "Attention: Annouces classees." English is widely understood.

GREECE

Akropolis, 12 Phidiou St., Athens.
Eleftherotypia, 57 Panepistimiou St., Athens.
Ta Nea, 3 Christou Lada Str. Athens.
Vradini, 9 Pireos St., Athens.
Address your envelope to the classified ad department as follows: "Mikres Aggelies."

GUATEMALA

Diario de Centro America, 18 calle, 6-72, zona 1, Guatemala, Guatemala.
El Grafico, 14 Avenida, 4-33, zona 1, Guatemala, Guatemala.
La Hora, 9a. calle "A," 1-56, zona 1, Guatemala, Guatemala.
Prensa Libre, 13 calle, 9-31, zona 1, Guatemala, Guatemala.

GUYANA

The Guyana Chronicle, Lama Avenue, Bel Air Park, Greater Georgetown, Guyana, South America.
The official language is English.

ICELAND

Morgundladid, Adalstraeti 6, 101 Reykjavik.
Dagbladid Visir, Sidumuli 12-14, 105 Reykjavik.
Dagbladid NT, Sidumuli 15, 105 Reykjavik.
Thodviljinn, Sidumuli 6, 105 Reykjavik.
Letters written in English will be understood by newspaper staffs.

INDIA

Indian Express (English), Bahadur Shah Zafar Marg, New Delhi.
Nav Bharat Times, Bahadur Shah Zafar Marg, New Delhi.
Times of India (English), Bahadur Sha Zafar Marg, New Delhi.
The Hindu (English), Madras, Tamil Nadu.
The most widely spoken language is Hindi. Letters in English will be understood.

INDONESIA

The Indonesia Observer, Jalan A.M. Sangaji 11, Jakarta Pusat. Tele: 344642.
The Indonesia Times Daily (English), Jalan Letnan Jenderal S. Parman Kav. N. 72 P.O. Box 224. Tele: 348170 or 350113.
Kompas Daily, Jalan Palmerah Selatan 26-28 P.O. Box 615, Jakarta Barat.
Sinar Harapan Daily, Jalan Dewi Sartika 136D. P.O. Box 260, Jakarta Timur. Tele: 884372 or 881274.
Official language is Indonesian with English the second most common language. Letters written in English will be understood by newspaper staffs.

IRELAND

Belfast

Belfast Telegraph, 124-132 Royal Ave., Belfast.

Cork

Cork Examiner, 95 Patrick St., Cork.

Dublin
Irish Independent, 90 Middle Abbey St., Dublin.
The Irish Press, Irish Press House, Dublin.
English is the most widely spoken language in Ireland.

ISRAEL

Jerusalem: The Jerusalem Post, Romema, Jerusalem.
Tel Aviv: Maariv, 2 Karlibach St., Tel Aviv.

ITALY

Milano

Corriere della Sera, Milano (20121), via Solferino 28.

Roma

la Repubblica, Roma (00100), p. zza Indipendenza 11/B.
Paese Sera, Roma (00187), via del Tritone 61/62 Galleria INA.

Torino

Stampa Sera, Torino (10126), v. Marenco 32.
Note: Address your envelope to the classified ad department as follows: "Ufficio Pubblicita."

JAPAN

Asahi Evening News (English), Asahi Evening News-sha, 7-8-5, Tsukiji, Chui-ku, Tokyo 104.
Japan Times (English edition for Osaka area), Nakanoshima Saiwai Bldg., 3-1, Nakanoshima 2-chome, Kita-ku, Osaka 530. Tele: 06 202 3591.
Japan Times (English edition for Tokyo area), 5-4, Shibaura 4-chome, Minato-ku, Tokyo 108. Tele: 03 453 5311.
Mainichi Shimbun, Mainichi Shimbun-sha, 1-1-1, Hitotsubashi, Chiyoda-ku, Tokyo 100.

JORDAN

Al-Dustour, P.O. Box 591, Jordan Press and Publishing Company, Amman. Tele: 0664153.
Al-Rai, P.O. Box 6710, Jordan Press Foundation, University Road, Amman. Tele: 06671714.

Jerusalem Star (English), P.O. Box 591, Jordan Press and Publishing Company, Amman. Tele: 06641534, or 06641312.
Jordan Times (English), P.O. Box 6710, Jordan Press Foundation, University Road, Amman. Tele: 0666320.
Official language is Arabic but English is widely understood.

KUWAIT
Al-Rai Al-Aam, Kuwait City.
Al-Seyassah, Kuwait City.
Arab Times (English), Kuwait City.
Kuwait Times (English), Kuwait City.
Arabic is the official language, but letters written in English will likely be understood.

LUXEMBOURG
Luxemburger Wort, 2 R. Christophe, Plantin, Luxembourg-Gasperich.

MADAGASCAR
Madagascar-Matin, 1 Lalana Solombavambahoaka Frantsay, 77 Antsahavola, Antananarivo. Tele: 212-41.
Lakroan' i Madagasikara, Tranoprinty Md. Paoly Ambatomena, B.P. 1169 Fianarantsoa. Tele: 5514-41.
ATRIKA, Direction de la Presse Antaninarenina, Antananarivo. Tele: 201-06.
Most common languages written and spoken are Malagasy and French but most journalists at these newspapers can understand English.

MALAYSIA
Kuala Lumpur
The New Straits Times (English), 31 Jalan Riong, Kuala Lumpur. Tele: 03 445 444.
Utusan Malaysia, 46-M Jalan Lima, off Jalan Chan Sow Lin, Kuala Lumpur. Tele: 03 288 422.
Berita Harian, 31 Jalan Riong, Kuala Lumpur. Tele: 03 445 444.

Selangor
The Star (English), 13 Jalan 13/16, Petaling Jaya, Selangor. Tele: 03 578 811.

MEXICO
Acapulco: Avance, Costera Miguel Aleman #187 — 1er, Piso.
Cuernavaca: Diario De Morelos, Morelos Sur #1201 Cuernavaca.
Guadalajara: El Occidental, Calz, Independencia Sur 324, P.O.B. 1-699, Guadalajara.
Mexico City: Novedades, Av. Morelos No. 16-50 (5th fl) 1 D.F.
Monterrey: El Norte, Washington 629 Ote., Apdo, Postal 186, Monterrey.

MOROCCO

Casablanca

Le Matin du Sahara (French), rue Mohamed Smiha, Casablanca. Tele: 712 71.

Rabat

Al-Alam, 11 Boulevard Allal Ben Abdallah, Rabat. Tele: 260 11 or 324 19.
Al Ittihad Al Ichtiraki, Rue de Medina, Rabat. Tele: 264 64.
L'Opinion (French), 11 Boulevard Alla Ben Abdallah, Rabat. Tele: 279 12 or 279 13.
Dominant languages are Arabic, French, and Spanish. Letters written in English might be understood.

NETHERLANDS

Amsterdam

de Telegraaf, Postbus 376, Amsterdam.
de Volkskrant, Postbus 1002, Amsterdam.

Rotterdam

Algemeen Dagblad, Postbus 241, Rotterdam.

Haag

Haagsche Courant, Postbus 16050, 2500AA den Haag.

NEW ZEALAND

Auckland: New Zealand Herald, Wilson & Horton Ltd., Box 32, 149 Queen St., Auckland.
Christchurch: The Press, Christ Church Press Co. Ltd., P.O. Box 1005, Cathedral Square, Christchurch.
Dunedin: Otago Daily Times, Otago Daily Times & Witness Newspaper Co. Ltd., P.O. Box 181, Stuart St., Dunedin.
Hamilton: Waikatq Times, Box 444, Tasman St., Te Rapa, Hamilton.

NORWAY

Oslo

Aftenposten, Akersgaten 51, Boks 1178/Sentrum, Oslo 1.
Dagbladet, Boks 116, Sentrum, Oslo 1.

PAKISTAN
Islamabad: The Muslim (English), 9 Hameed Chambers, Aabpara, Islamabad. Tele: 8102796.
Karachi: Dawn (English), Dr. Ziauddin Ahmed Road, Karachi. Tele: 516761.
Lahore: Pakistan Times, The Pakistan Times Press, Lahore. Tele: 66027.
Rawalpindi: Jang, The Daily Jang, Rawalpindi. Tele: 70223.
Letters written in English will be understood by newspaper staffs.

PANAMA
La Estrella de Panama, Apartado 159, Panama 1, Republica de Panama.
La Republica, Apartado 165, Panama 1, Republica de Panama.
La Critica, Apartado B-4, Panama 9A, Republica de Panama.
Letters written in English will be understood by newspaper staffs.

PERU
El Comercio, Jr. A. Miro Quesada 300, Lima 1. Tele: 28-7620.
Expreso-Extra, Jr. Ica 646, Lima 1. Tele: 28-7470.
La Republica, Jr. Camana 320, Lima 1. Tele 27-6455 or 27-1724.
El Peruano, (Diario Oficial), Jr. Quilca 556, Lima 1. Tele: 23-5263.
Dominant languages are Castellano and Quechua but a letter written in English will be understood by newspaper staff and others.

PHILIPPINES
Bulletin Today, Recoletos St. cor. Muralla St., Intramuros, Manila. Tele: 47 15 51.
Daily Express, 371 Bonifacio Drive, Port Area, Manila. Tele: 47 82 61.
Times Journal, Railroad and 19th Streets, Port Area, Manila. Tele: 48 75 11 or 48 75 26.
Letters written in English will be understood by newspaper staffs.

PORTUGAL
Lisbon: O Seculo, Rua do Secula-41, Lisbon.
Porto: O Primeiro De Janeiro, Rua de Santa Catarina, 326, Porto.
Letters written in English will usually be understood by newspaper staffs.

PUERTO RICO
San Juan: El Nuevo Dia, P.O. Box S-297, San Juan.

SAUDI ARABIA
Dammam
Al-Yaum, Near Coast Guard Offices, P.O. Box 565, Dammam. Tele: 833 1091 or 833 1906.

Jeddah

Al-Madina, Kilo 5, Makkah Road, P.O. Box 807, Jeddah. Tele: 689 5168 or 688 0344.
Arab News (English), Arab News Bldg., off Sharafia, P.O. Box 4556, Jeddah. Tele: 653 4239 or 653 3723.
Saudi Gazette (English), Okaz Est., Mina Road, P.O. Box 5576, Jeddah. Tele: 667 4020 or 667 4408.

Makkah

Al-Nadwa, Al-Juffali Building, Al-Ghazza, Makkah. Tele: 542 3048 or 574 8150.

Riyadh

Al-Jazeerah, Al-Nasirya Street, P.O. Box 354, Riyadh. Tele: 402 1440 or 403 3361.
Official language is Arabic but letters in English will be understood.

SCOTLAND

Aberdeen: Evening Express, P.O. Box 43, Lang Stracht, Mastrick, Aberdeen.

SOUTH AFRICA

Johannesburg

Rapport, P.O. Box 8422, Johannesburg.
Sunday Times (English), SA Associated Newspapers Ltd., P.O. Box 1090, Johannesburg.

Port Elizabeth

Eastern Province Herald (English), P.O. Box 1117, Port Elizabeth.

Pretoria

Hoofstad, P.O. Box 422, Pretoria.
Pretoria News (English), P.O. Box 439, Pretoria.

SOUTH KOREA

Chosun Ilbo-61, 1-ga, Taepyong-ro, Chung-gu, Seoul. Tele: 03 725 6611.

Dong-A Ilbo-139, Sejong-ro, Chongno-gu, Seoul. Tele: 03 723 5221.
Hankook Ilbo-14, Chunghak-dong, Chongno-gu, Seoul. Tele: 03 722 4151.
Korea Herald (English) 1-12, 3-ga, Hoehyon-dong, Chung-gu, Seoul. Tele: 03 756 7711.
Korea Times (English) 14, Chunghak-dong, Chongno-gu, Seoul. Tele: 03 722 4151.

SPAIN

Barcelona: La Vanguardia, Pelayo 28, Barcelona 1.
Cordoba: Cordoba, Ingeniero Juan de la Cieva, 18 (Pol. Industrial de la Torrecilla), Cordoba.
Madrid: ABC, Prensa Espanola SA, Serrano 61, Madrid 6.
Sevilla: ABC, Cardenal Illundain, 9, Apartado Postale 49, Sevilla.

SWEDEN

Karlstad: NYA Wermlands Tidningen, Box 28, 651/02 Karlstad.
Orebro: Nerikes Allehanda, Box 1603, 701/16 Orebro.
Malmo: Sydsvenske Dagbladet, Box 145, 201/21 Malmo.
Stockholm: Expressen, Gjorwellsgatan 30, 105/16 Stockholm.

SWITZERLAND

Zurich: Neue Zuercher Zeitung, Postfach, 8021 Zurich.
Geneva: Journal De Geneve, Case postale 439, 1211 Geneva 11.
Bern: Bund, Effingerstrasse 1, 3011 Bern.
Basel: Basler Zeitung, St. Alban-Anlage 14, 4052 Basel.
NOTE: The advertising agency S.R.W.-P.R.I. International Inc., 1560 Broadway, Room 1300, New York, NY 10036, telephone 212 575-9292, represents Publicitas SA, 1002 Lausanne, in Switzerland, which represents several Swiss newspapers, and can place your classified ads for you.

TRINIDAD AND TOBAGO

Trinidad Guardian, Trinidad Publishing Company, Ltd., 22-24 St. Vincent St., Port of Spain, Trinidad. Tele: 809 623-8870.
Trinidad Express, 35 Independence Square, Port of Spain, Trinidad. Tele: 809 623-1711.
The Evening News, Trinidad Publishing Company, Ltd., 22-24 St. Vincent St., Port of Spain, Trinidad. Tele: 809 523-8879.

TURKEY

Cumhuriyet Gazetesi, Turkocagi Caddesi, Cagaloglu-Istanbul. Tele: 520 9703.
Hurriyet Gazetesi, Cagaloglu-Istanbul. Tele: 526 2000.
Milliyet Gazetesi, Nuruosmaniye Cad. No. 65, Cagaloglu-Istanbul. Tele: 522 4410.
Tercuman Gazetesi, Londra Asfalti, Topkapi-Istanbul. Tele: 524 4210.
Letters written in English will be understood by newspaper staffs.

UGANDA

Munnansi, P.O. Box 1658, Kampala. Tele: 259682.
Uganda Times, P.O. Box 20081, Kampala. Tele: 234403.
English is Uganda's official language.

UNITED STATES
ALABAMA
Birmingham: Birmingham News, 2200 North 4th Ave., Birmingham, AL 35202.

ALASKA
Anchorage: Anchorage Times, Box 40, Anchorage, AK 99510.

ARIZONA
Phoenix: Phoenix Republic, 120 E. Van Buren St. Phoenix, AZ 85004.

ARKANSAS
Little Rock: Arkansas Gazette, 112 W. Third Ave., Little Rock, AR 72203.

CALIFORNIA
Long Beach: Independent, Press Telegram, 604 Pine Ave., Long Beach, CA 90844.
Los Angeles: Los Angeles Times, Times Mirror Square, Los Angeles, CA 90053.

Sacramento: Sacramento Bee, 21st & Q, Sacramento, CA 95852.
San Diego: San Diego Union, 350 Camino de la Reina, San Diego, CA 92108.
San Francisco: San Francisco Chronicle, 925 Mission St., San Francisco, CA 94103.
San Jose: San Jose Mercury News, 750 Ridder Park Dr., San Jose, CA 95131.
Santa Ana: Santa Ana Register, 625 N. Grand Ave., Santa Ana, CA 92711.

COLORADO
Denver: Denver Post, 650 15 St., Denver, CO 80201.

CONNECTICUT
Hartford: Hartford Courant, 285 Broad St., Hartford, CT 06115.

DISTRICT OF COLUMBIA
Washington, DC: Washington Post, 1150 15th St., N.W., Washington, DC 20071.

FLORIDA
Fort Lauderdale: Fort Lauderdale Sun-Sentinel, 101 N. New River Dr., East, Ft. Lauderdale, FL 33302.
Jacksonville: Florida Times-Union, 1 Riverside Ave., Jacksonville, FL 32202.
Orlando: Orlando Sentinel, 633 N. Orange Ave., Orlando, FL 32801.
St. Petersburg: St. Petersburg Times, P.O. Box 1121, 490 First Ave., South, St. Petersburg, FL 33731.
Tampa: Tampa Tribune, Box 191, 202 S. Parker, Tampa, FL 33601.

GEORGIA
Atlanta: Atlanta Journal/Atlanta Constitution, 72 Marietta St., N.W., Atlanta, GA 30303.

HAWAII
Honolulu: Honolulu Star-Bulletin, 605 Kapiolani Blvd., Honolulu, HI 96801.

IDAHO
Grangeville: Idaho County Free Press, Box 267, Grangeville, ID 83530.

ILLINOIS
Chicago: Chicago Tribune, 435 N. Michigan Ave., Chicago, IL 60611.
Peoria: Peoria Journal-Star, 1 News Plaza, Peoria, IL 61601.

INDIANA
Evansville: Evansville Courier & Press, 201 N.W. 2nd St., Evansville, IN 47701.
Indianapolis: Indianapolis Star, 307 N. Pennsylvania St., Indianapolis, IN 46206.
South Bend: South Bend Tribune, 223 W. Colfax, South Bend, IN 46626.

IOWA
Des Moines: Des Moines Register, 715 Locust St., Des Moines, IA 50304.

KANSAS
Wichita: Wichita Eagle, 825 East Douglas St., Wichita, KS 67201.

KENTUCKY
Louisville: Louisville Courier-Journal, 525 W. Broadway, Louisville, KY 40202.

LOUISIANA
New Orleans: The Times-Picayune, 3800 Howard Ave., New Orleans, LA 70140.

MAINE
Belfast: The Republican Journal, 4 Main, Box 327, Belfast, ME 04915.

MARYLAND
Baltimore: Baltimore Sun, Calvert & Center Sts., Baltimore, MD 21203.

MASSACHUSETTS
Boston: Boston Herald American, 300 Harrison Ave., Boston, MA 02106.
Springfield: Springfield Republican, P.O. Box 1131, Springfield, MA 01101.
Worcester: Worcester Telegram, The Evening Gazette Sunday Telegram, 20 Franklin St., Worcester MA 01613.

MICHIGAN
Detroit: Detroit News, 615 Lafayette Blvd., Detroit, MI 48231.
Flint: The Flint Journal, 200 E. 1st St., Flint, MI 48502.
Grand Rapids: The Grand Rapids Press, Press Plaza-Vandenberg Center, Grand Rapids, MI 49502.

MINNESOTA
Minneapolis: Minneapolis Tribune, 427 Portland Ave., Minneapolis, MN 55488.
St. Paul: St. Paul Pioneer Press, 55 E. 4th St., St. Paul, MN 55101.

MISSISSIPPI
Jackson: Clarion-Ledger & News, 311 E. Pearl St., Jackson, MS 39205.

MISSOURI
Kansas City: Kansas City Star, 1729 Grand Ave., Kansas City, MO 64108.
St. Louis: St. Louis Globe-Democrat, 710 N. Tucker Blvd., St. Louis, MO 63101.

NEBRASKAOmaha: Omaha World-Herald, World-Herald Square, Omaha, NE 68102.

NEW HAMPSHIRE
Nashua: 1590 Broadcaster, 502 W. Hollis St., Box 548, Nashua, NH 03061.

NEW JERSEY
Camden: Camden Courier-Post, Camden, NJ 08101.
Hackensack: Hackensack Bergen Record, 150 River St., Hackensack, NJ 07602.
Newark: Newark Star-Ledger, Court & Plaine Sts., Newark, NJ 07101.

NEW MEXICO

Albuquerque: The Albuquerque Journal, P.O. Drawer J. Albuquerque, NM 87112.

NEW YORK

Buffalo: Buffalo News, One News Plaza, Buffalo, NY 14240.
Garden City: Newsday, 550 Stewart Ave., Garden City, NY 11530.
New York: New York Daily News, 220 East 42nd St., New York, NY 10017.
New York: (national distribution): **The Wall Street Journal,** 22 Cortlandt St., New York, NY 10007.
Rochester: Rochester Democrat & Chronicle, 55 Exchange St., Rochester, NY 14614.
Syracuse: Syracuse Herald-American, Clinton Square, Syracuse, NY 13201.
West Hampton: Suffolk Life Newspaper Group, Montauk Highway, West Hampton, NY 11977.

NORTH CAROLINA

Charlotte: The Charlotte Observer, 600 S. Tryon St., Box 32188, Charlotte, NC 28232.

OHIO

Akron: Akron Beacon Journal, 44 E. Exchange St., Akron, OH 44328.
Cincinnati: Cincinnati Enquirer, 617 Vine St., Cincinnati, OH 45202.
Cleveland: Cleveland Plain Dealer, 1801 Superior Ave. N.E., Cleveland, OH 44114.
Columbus: Columbus Dispatch, 34 S. Third St., Columbus, OH 43216.
Dayton: Dayton News, 4th & Ludlow Sts., Dayton, OH 45401.
Toledo: Toledo Blade, 541 Superior St., Toledo, OH 43660.
Youngstown: Youngstown Vindicator, Vindicator Square, Youngstown, OH 44501.

OKLAHOMA

Oklahoma City: Daily Oklahoman, 500 North Broadway, Box 25125, Oklahoma City, OK 73125.
Tulsa: Tulsa World, 315 S. Boulder Ave., Box 1770, Tulsa, OK 74102.

OREGON
Portland: **The Oregonian**, 1320 S.W. Broadway, Portland, OR 97201.

PENNSYLVANIA
Allentown: **Allentown Call-Chronical**, 6th & Linden Sts., Alllentown, PA 18105.
Philadelphia: **The Philadelphia Inquirer**, 400 No. Broad St., Philadelphia, PA 19101.
Pittsburgh: **Pittsburg Press**, Box 566, Pittsburgh, PA 15230.

RHODE ISLAND
Providence: **Providence Bulletin**, 75 Fountain St., Providence, RI 02902.

SOUTH CAROLINA
Columbia: **Columbia State**, Stadium Rd., P.O. Box 1333, Columbia, SC 29202.

SOUTH DAKOTA
Sioux Falls: **Sioux Falls Argus Leader**, 200 S. Minnesota Ave., Sioux Falls, SD 57102.

TENNESSEE
Knoxville: **The News-Sentinel**, 204 W. Church Ave., Knoxville, TN 37901.
Memphis: **The Commercial Appeal**, 495 Union Ave., Memphis, TN 38101.
Nashville: **Nashville Tennessean**, 1100 Broadway, Nashville, TN 37202.

TEXAS
Dallas: **The Dallas Morning News**, Communications Center, Dallas, TX 75265.
Ft. Worth: **Ft. Worth Star-Telegram**, P.O. Box 1870, Ft. Worth, TX 76101.
Houston: **Houston Chronicle**, 801 Texas Ave., Houston, TX 77002.
San Antonio: **San Antonio Light**, Box 161, McCullough & Broadway, San Antonio, TX 78291.

UTAH
Salt Lake City: **Salt Lake City Tribune**, 143 So. Main St., Salt Lake City, UT 84110.

VERMONT
Manchester Center: **Times of Manchester**, P.O. Box 1265, Manchester Center, VT 05255.

VIRGINIA
Norfolk: The Virginian-Pilot, 150 W. Brambleton Ave., Norfolk, VA 23501.
Richmond: Richmond Times-Dispatch, 333 East Grace St., Richmond, VA 23219
Roanoke: Roanoke Times & World News, 201-209 W. Campbell Ave., Box 2491, Roanoke, VA 24010.

WASHINGTON
Seattle: Seattle Times, Fairview Ave. N. & Johs St., Seattle, WA 98111.
Tacoma: Tacoma News Tribune, Box 11000, 1950 S. State St., Tacoma, WA 98411.

WEST VIRGINIA
Charleston: Charleston Daily Mail, 1001 Virginia St., E., Box 2993, Charleston, WV 25330.

WISCONSIN
Milwaukee: The Milwaukee Journal, 333 W. State St., Milwaukee, WI 53201.

VIRGIN ISLANDS
Charlotte Amalie: Virgin Islands Daily News, P.O. Box 1510, U.S. Virgin Islands 00801.
Christiansted: St. Croix Avis, P.O. Box 750, Christiansted, St. Croix, U.S. Virgin Islands, 00820.

WEST GERMANY
Bonn: Die Welt, Godesberger Allee 99, 5300 Bonn 2. Tele: 0228 3041.
Frankfurt: Frankfurter Allgemeine, Postfach 29 01, 6000 Frankfurt am Main. Tele: 069 75910.
Frankfurt: Frankfurter Rundschau, Grobe Eschenheimer Str. 16,6000 Frankfurt a. M. Tele: 0611 21991.
Munchen: Suddeutsche Zeitung, Postfach 20 22 20, 8000 Munchen. Tele: 089 21830.
Letters addressed in English will be understood by newspaper staffs.

YUGOSLAVIA
Beograd: Politica, Makedonska 29, 11000 Beograd. Tele: 011 332 300, or 011 325 761, or 011 324 1919.
Sarajevo: Oslobodjenje, Dzemala Bijedica 185, 71000 Sarajevo.
Skopje: Ro Nip Nova Makedonija, OOZT Mraketing, Ul. Mito Hadzivasilev, Jasmin bb, 91000 Skopje.
Zagreb: OOUR Vjesnik, Avenija bratstva i jedinstva 4, 41000 Zagreb.
Letters written in English will be understood by newspaper staffs.

COMMUNITY HOST AND INTERNATIONAL VISITOR SERVICES

ENGLAND

Academic Travel (Lowestoft) Ltd., The Briar School of English, 8 Gunton Cliff, Lowestoft, Suffolk NR32 4PE.
At Home, 64 Kingsley Way, London N2 OEW.
The Central Bureau for Educational Visits and Exchanges, 44 Baker St., London W1M 2HJ.
Country Cousins International Agency, Moorings, Watermouth, Ilfracombe, Devon.
Family Friendship Association, "Brecon," Chyngton Rd., Seaford, East Sussex BN25 4HH.
The Florentine Bureau, Associated with the Ann Shaw Agency, 9 Tower Rd., Orpington, Kent.
International Friendship League, "Peace Haven," 3 Creswick Rd., Acton, London W3 9HE.
Mauder Associates, 55 High St., Braintree, Essex CM7 5JX.
PARVO, c/o The Central Bureau for Educational Visits and Exchanges, 43 Dorset St., London W1H 3FN.
Robert Lawson and Associates Ltd., The Butts, Great Budworth, Northwich, Cheshire.

UNITED STATES
ALABAMA

Birmingham Council for International Visitors, 2027 First Ave., N Suite 300, Birmingham AL 35203.
Huntsville-Madison Council For International Visitors, Madison County Courthouse Rm. 525, Huntsville AL 35801.
Rotary Club of Tuscaloosa, P.O. Box 833, University of Alabama, University AL 35486.

ARKANSAS

Arkansas Council for International Visitors, 230 State Capitol, Little Rock AR 72201.

CALIFORNIA

Community Committee for International Students, Stanford University, Box 5816, Stanford CA 94305.
Friends of the International Center, University of California, San Diego, Q-018, La Jolla CA 92093.
Hospitality for Overseas Students & Travelers, 562 Hudson St., Redwood City CA 94062.
Hospitality International, 500 Lucas Ave., Suite 104, Los Angeles CA 90017.
International Community Council, 1250 Bellflower Blvd., Long Beach CA 90840.
International Hospitality Center, 312 Sutter St., San Francisco CA 94108.
International House, University of California, Berkeley, Berkeley CA 94720.
International Student Services, 1553 N. Hudson Ave., Los Angeles CA 90028.

COLORADO

Friends of International Students, Colorado Sem, University of Denver, Denver CO 80208.
International Center, Inc., 14 Palmer House, Fort Collins CO 80521.
International Hospitality Center, 980 Grant St., Denver CO 80203.

CONNECTICUT

International Institute of Connecticut, 480 E. Washington Ave., Bridgeport CT 06608.
World Affairs Center, 1380 Asylum Ave., Hartford CT 06105.
International Center, 442 Temple St., P.O. Box 94A, New Haven CT 06520

DELAWARE

Delaware Council for International Visitors, Inc., 910 Gilpin St., Box 831, Wilmington DE 19899.

DISTRICT OF COLUMBIA

The Hospitality & Information Service, 1630 Crescent Pl., NW, Washington DC 20009.
International Student Advisory Services, Inc., 3000 Connecticut Ave., NW, Suite 140, Washington DC 20008.
International Student House, 1825 R St., NW, Washington DC 20009.
International Visitors Information Service, 801 19th St., NW, Washington DC 20006.
Washington International Center, 1630 Crescent Pl., NW, Washington DC 20009.

FLORIDA

Council for International Visitors of Greater Miami, Olympic Bldg. Suite 806, 174 E Flagler, Miami FL 33131.
Gainsville Council for International Friendship, P.O. Box 12369, Gainesville FL 23604.
International Exchange Host Family Program, 212 Bryan Hall Florida St. University, Tallahassee FL 32306.
Mid Florida Council for International Visitors, P.O. Box 1311, Winter Park FL 32790.

GEORGIA

Atlanta Council for International Visitors, 1112 Peachtree St., Atlanta GA 30309.
East-West Foundation, Inc., P.O. Box 10067, Atlanta GA 30319.

HAWAII

Friends of the East-West Center, 1777 East-W Road, Honolulu HI 96848.

ILLINOIS

International Visitors Center of Chicago, 116 S Michigan Ave., Rm 1200, Chicago IL 60603.
Macomb Host Family Program, 100 Mem Hall, Niu, Macomb IL 61455.
Peoria Area Friends of International Students, Bradley University, Peoria IL 61625.
Springfield Commission On International Visitors, 2100 Cherry Rd., Springfield IL 62704.

INDIANA

Bloomington Community Hospitality Committee, Indiana University, Bloomington IN 47401.

IOWA

Des Moines Area Council for International Understanding, 2838 University Ave., Des Moines IA 50311.

KANSAS

Small World, Inc., 2415 W 23rd St., Lawrence KS 66044.

LOUISIANA

International Hospitality Foundation, International Student Center, Louisiana St. University, Baton Rouge LA 70803.

MASSACHUSETTS

Host Family Program, 1350 Massachusetts Ave., Rm 858, Cambridge MA 02138.
Host To International Students Program, Massachusetts Institute of Technology, Rm 10342, Cambridge MA 02139.
International Center of Worcester, 18 Beaver St., Worcester MA 01603.
International Institute of Boston, Inc., 287 Commonwealth Ave., Boston MA 02115.
World Affairs Council, 22 Batterymarch St., Boston MA 02109.

MICHIGAN

Ann Arbor Public Schools, 2555 S State Rd., Ann Arbor MI 48104.
International Institute of Metropolitan Detroit, 111 E Kirby Ave., Detroit MI 48202.
Viva International Student Services, 719 Griswold, Suite 2215, Detroit MI 48226.
Volunteers for International Hospitality Program, 603 E Madison, Ann Arbor MI 48109.

MINNESOTA

International Club, College of St Theresa, Winona MN 55987.
International Students, Inc., 1240 Thomas Ave., Saint Paul MN 55104.
Minnesota International Center, 711 E River Rd., Minneapolis MN 55455.

Minnesota International Center, 2732 Upton Ave. S, Minneapolis MN 55416.

MISSISSIPPI

International Woman's Club, 212 Hiwasse Dr., Starkville MS 39759.

MISSOURI

Friendship International — Baptist Church, Hanley Rd., 7701 Maryland, St. Louis MO 63105.
People to People, 2440 Pershing Rd., Suite G 30, Kansas City MO 64108.

MONTANA

Bozeman Friends of International Students, Box 1018, Belgrade MT 59714.

NEBRASKA

Grand Island Council for International Visitors, 821 S Authur, Grand Island NE 68801.

NEW MEXICO

Council On International Relations, P.O. Box 1223, Santa Fe NM 87501.

NEW YORK

Buffalo World Hospitality Association, Inc., 107 Delaware Ave., 205 Statler, Buffalo NY 14202.

NORTH CAROLINA

Coordinating Council for International People, UNCC, Charlotte NC 28223.
Greensboro Coordinating Committee for Foreign Students, Greensboro Chamber of Commerce, Greensboro NC 32604.
Host Family Program, Carolina Union 065A — UNC, Chapel Hill NC 27514.

OHIO

American Friend Families, Youngstown State University, Youngstown OH 44503.

Cleveland Council On World Affairs, 601 Rockwell Ave., Cleveland OH 44114.
Council of International Programs, 1001 Huron Rd., Suite 209, Cleveland OH 44315.
Hosting International Travelers, 520 Meredith Ln., Apt. 201, Cuyahoga Falls OH 44223.
International Visitors Center, 105 W Fourth St., Rm. 822, Cincinnati OH 45202.

OREGON

Community Volunteers for International Students, 19600 S Molalla Ave., Oregon City OR 97045.
Crossroads International, Inc., Oregon St. University, Ads A100, Corvallis OR 97331.
Foundation for International Services, Inc., P.O. Box 230278, Portland OR 97223.
World Affairs Council, 1912 SW Sixth Ave., Portland OR 97201.

PENNSYLVANIA

Community International Hospitality Council, Pennsylvania St. University, 111 Kern Bldg., University Park PA 16802.
Council for International Service & Hospitality, 56 W Elizabeth Ave., Bethlehem PA 18018.
International Community Hospitality Council, 172 W Prospect Ave, State College PA 16801.
International House of Philadelphia, 3701 Chestnut St., Philadelphia PA 19104.
Pittsburgh Council for International Visitors, 139 University Pl., 363 Mervis Hall, Pittsburgh PA 15260.

RHODE ISLAND

International House of Rhode Island, 8 Stimson Ave., Providence RI 02906.

SOUTH CAROLINA

Columbia Council for Internationals, 1470 Greenhill Rd., Columbia SC 29206.

TENNESSEE

International Friends, 757 Court, Memphis TN 38105.

TEXAS

Dallas Committee for Foreign Visitors, 9417 Waterview Rd., Dallas TX 75218.
Houston International Service Committee, 5622 Briar Dr., Houston TX 77056.
International Hospitality Committee, Drawer A, University Station, Austin TX 78712.

UTAH

International Visitors Utah Council, Hotel Utah, Salt Lake City UT 84111.

WASHINGTON

International Advisory Services, P.O. Box 583, Mukilteo WA 98275.
Pacific Northwest International, 1701 Broadway, Seattle WA 98122.
Spokane International Exchange Council, Box 32, Liberty Lake WA 99019.

WISCONSIN

Host Family Program, 517 W Maple Ridge Dr., Stevens Point WI 54481.
International Institute of Milwaukee County, 2810 W Highland Blvd., Milwaukee WI 53208.
Madison Friends of International Students, 3426 Lake Mendota Rd., Madison WI 53705.

Appendix C

Home And Area Information List

It is a tremendous help to exchange partners coming to your home if you have prepared a list of essential and often used telephone numbers for emergency services, neighbors, transportation schedules, businesses, and area attractions. Such a list is ideally bound together with other information particular to your home, such as instructions on where the fuse box is and how appliances operate (operating instructions for complicated appliances also should be affixed to the units in question).

Following is a list that you can either get ideas from for writing your own list, or photocopy directly and insert names and telephone numbers to leave for your partner. For your own ease of transition, you might want to offer to send your partner a photocopy of this list for him to fill out and leave for you.

I've numbered items that have locations which your partners might need to find, such as neighbor's homes and department stores, so that you can attach a hand drawn or local printed street map and designate where each place is located by writing the corresponding numbers at the appropriate positions.

Home And Area Information List
(Numbers Indicate Locations on Street Maps)

Emergency Telephone Numbers

    Police:

    Fire:

1. Hospital:

2. Dentist:

    Local Information:

    Operator:

Neighbors

3. Primary Reference Person:

4.

5.

Transportation Services

6. Nearest gasoline station:

    Emergency start up or road service:

    Towing Service:

7. Garage where automobile is repaired:

   Airport Information:

   Bus Information:

8. City Long-Distance Bus Depot:

   City Subway/Rail Information:

9. Long-Distance Train Depot:

   Taxi:

   Limousine:

Local Businesses

10. Food Market:

11. Health Food Market:

12 Supermarkets:

13.

14. Department Stores:

15.

16 Shopping Malls, Fashion Districts:

17.

18.

19. Bakery:

20. Pharmacy:

21. Liquor Store:

22. Post Office:

23. Local Tourist Information Office:

24. Travel Agency:

25. Laundry Service:

26. Dry Cleaners:

27. Barber Shop:

28. Beauty Salon:

29. Foreign Currency Exchange:

30. Bank:

31. Camera and Film Shop:

32. Florist:

33. Candy Store:

34. Ice Cream Parlor:

35. Book, Magazine, and Newspaper Store:

36. Record Album and Tape Shop:

37. Video Cassette Rental Store:

    Insurance Agent:

Home Services
    Baby-Sitters:

    Maid:

    Gardener:

    Kitchen Appliance Repair:

    Washer and Dryer Repair:

    Television, VCR and Stereo Repair:

    Pool Cleaning:

    Plumbing Repair:

Gas and Electricity Company:

Telephone Repair:

Restaurants (Besides name and telephone number, designate type of food, formal/informal, price range)

38.

39.

40.

41.

42.

43.

44.

45.

46.

47.

Nightclubs, Dancing, Bars (Besides name and telephone number, designate style, formal/informal, price range)

48.

49.

50.

51.

52.

Entertainment

53. Country Club:

54. Movie Theaters:

55.

56. Live Theater:

57.

58. Concert Hall:

59. Sporting Complexes, Stadiums, Arenas:

60.

61. Golf Courses:

62.

63. Ice Skating:

64. Roller Skating:

65. Snow Skiing:

66. Horseback Riding:

67. Amusement Park:

68. Workout Gym, Spa:

Special Local Attractions

69.

70.